Endor

How rarely we feel able to speak of (both hands in writing openly of hers. This beautifully written book invites us to look closely at passages of Scripture, to interrogate them, to believe them with our minds as well as our hearts. It will get talked about, passed around, and recommended—in the mission community and in churches.

JULIA CAMERON
Former Director of Publishing, Lausanne Movement
Founder, Dictum Press

Sacred Courage is an engaging and encouraging resource for anyone struggling with fear which—let's be honest!—is *all* of us. In these pages, Betsy shares vulnerably about her own experiences with fear and death, avoiding trite answers or lecturing while continually pointing readers to the truth of the gospel. *Sacred Courage* is jam-packed with hard-won wisdom, biblical insight, practical help, and clear points of application. I highly recommend this book!

CAROLINE COBB
Singer-songwriter
Author, *Advent for Exiles*

"Dear heart, let's repent not of fear but of our responses to it. And let's start seeing our fear as a call to action—a place for faith to rise."

This book is, without a doubt, the best book I have ever read on the subject of fear in our lives, how it controls us, and what a biblically grounded response should look like. I highly recommend this book for all Christians who desire a deeper walk with God and freedom from life-controlling fear and anxiety.

ELISE FRASIER
Podcast Host, *Martyrs and Missionaries*

Fear, manifested in a variety of ways and for a plethora of reasons, is a harsh reality which people everywhere encounter. Flowing out of her own experience dealing with fear, Betsy Kirk addresses this reality in her book *Sacred Courage*. She skillfully unwraps the various issues and questions related to fear through a careful study of the Word of God. She powerfully concludes that the answers to the complexities of fear are ultimately found in our relationship with God and our trust in his person and his promises. It has been my privilege to serve alongside Betsy as her teammate in Indonesia. I therefore know that the important truths, which she so excellently communicates in this book, are truths upon which she daily relies as she serves cross-culturally. Therefore, I highly recommend this book.

DR. GREG GRIPENTROG
Former President, OC International

More than ever, people in my context are recognizing the crippling effect that fear has in their lives. Betsy gives us a treasure trove of wisdom about how to reframe our experiences of fear as opportunities to grow in trust and in Christian courage. And she does so with compelling vulnerability by sharing her own experiences of anxious fear. At every turn, Betsy directs our gaze to the Lord Jesus, the one who offers us the peace we so desperately crave.

MARY WILLSON HANNAH
Author, *Heavenly Minded*

Are you afraid? Most of us would have to answer "yes" to that question. And whether our fears are of snakes or financial failure or global disaster, they loom large over our lives. *Sacred Courage* is a helpful companion for the fearful; in its pages, Betsy Kirk teaches us to understand our fears rightly and then applies the comfort of God and his Word to the feelings that keep us up at night. Keep this book by your nightstand and let it lead you to rest your anxious heart in the Lord.

MEGAN HILL
Managing Editor, The Gospel Coalition
Author, *Contentment: Seeing God's Goodness*

I love this book! Betsy writes with raw honesty about the reality of fear in her life and its potential to control and crush her. And yet every page is full of wisdom about how to cope with this daily reality and even to thrive in and through it. Here is faith-filled, Scripture-soaked counsel, delivered with gentle warmth and humor. It will be a great help to fellow-strugglers and all who seek to help them.

VAUGHAN ROBERTS
Rector of St Ebbe's Church, Oxford

Sacred Courage

Thinking Biblically About Fear and Anxiety

Betsy Kirk

WILLIAM
CAREY
PUBLISHING

visit us at missionbooks.org

William Carey Publishing (WCP) publishes resources to shape and advance the missiological conversation in the world. We publish a broad range of thought-provoking books and do not necessarily endorse all opinions set forth here or in works referenced within this book.

The URLs included in this workbook are provided for personal use only and are current as of the date of publication, but the publisher disclaims any obligation to update them after publication.

Published by William Carey Publishing
10 W. Dry Creek Cir
Littleton, CO 80120 | www.missionbooks.org

William Carey Publishing is a ministry of Frontier Ventures
Pasadena, CA | www.frontierventures.org

Cover and Interior Designer: Mike Riester

ISBNs: 978-1-64508-615-4 (paperback)
      978-1-64508-617-8 (epub)

Printed Worldwide

29 28 27 26 25 1 2 3 4 5 IN

Library of Congress Control Number: 2024950070

Contents

For my children: Norah, Harriet, Hugh, and Walter.
Whatever comes, may you always cling to Jesus
and walk securely in the love of your heavenly Father.

And for my father, who encouraged me to write this book.
Though he did not live to read it, he lived what it says.

Introduction

> "It's a dangerous business, Frodo, going out your door," he used to say. "You step into the Road, and if you don't keep your feet, there is no knowing where you might be swept off to. Do you realize that this is the very path that goes through Mirkwood, and that if you let it, it might take you to the Lonely Mountain or even further and to worse places?" —J. R. R. Tolkien, *The Fellowship of the Ring*

A key premise of this book is that everyone, at some level, is afraid. Though the specific fears we feel most, the way we express them, and even our awareness of them differ as widely as our personalities, every human inhabitant of earth experiences fear. Perhaps, either always or for a season, you have known a life burdened by dread. You know well that inner tightness, the brittleness of heart, that comes when you are afraid to face the future. Perhaps you would claim you're "not a fearful person," but if you are honest with yourself, if you truly begin to ask internally what could make you feel fear, you find buried areas that you don't like to think about or "what if" questions you don't dare consider. Either way, this book is written for you. It also may be that you have wrestled with fear and found victory, that Christ has weakened the hold of fear on your life in your current season. If so, the church needs you. I pray this book may still help you realize fully *why* you are not afraid and help you remind us of it.

Fear has had its teeth in my own life as long as I can remember. It has been a pronounced struggle in my spiritual journey. I've been a Christian since I was a young child, and as I've grown up into Christ, wrestling with fear has been a catalyst for the growth of my faith. That is probably my only qualification for writing this book. I am not a clinical psychologist or a trained counselor. I'm not an expert in anything except perhaps the novels of Jane Austen or how to poach an egg. But when it comes to what the battle with fear looks like in the Christian heart, I have probably earned at least a PhD.

God's unique plan for my life has presented me with many challenges in this area as he has led my husband and me to foreign places, encountering different risks than we would face at home. At each one of my shaky steps on this journey, God has been right there, faithfully revealing himself to my doubting heart and always, always being the solid rock under my feet. This book is not my personal wisdom; it is simply my effort to share what God has done. It would be fair to say that I have learned every lesson in this book the hard way.

My desire in writing my own story is that my voice would join the chorus of many other voices of the past and present, the great "cloud of witnesses," who can testify to God's shepherding of his people through a scary world. Often, I have been profoundly encouraged by the writings of others. The Roman poet Horace offered excellent advice centuries ago: one should "interrogate the writings of the wise, asking them to tell you how you can get through your life in a peaceable tranquil way."[1] I have been helped by the writings of Lilias Trotter, Elisabeth Elliot, Corrie ten Boom, C. S. Lewis, Eugene Peterson, and many others. I owe most, perhaps, to Charles Spurgeon. A few years ago, following a heavy catastrophe in my life, my dear mother suggested that I read his massive commentary on the Psalms, *The Treasury of David*. As I did so, Spurgeon's illuminating insights, his faithful exhortations, and especially his pastoral care supported me through a season of the most intense spiritual wrestling I have yet known. Much of the fruit of that time I have endeavored to share in these pages.

Thus this book's aim is to offer you, through personal story, reflection, and meditation on Scripture, what I have received from the

---

1 I am indebted to Alan Jacob's recent book *Breaking Bread with the Dead* for this quote. I have relied so heavily on Christian writers of the past that an alternate title for this book could be *Facing Fear with the Dead*.

Lord. I hope it will illustrate how embracing the truths about God as gleaned from the Bible and a growing relationship with Jesus Christ can comfort and empower believers who are afraid. It strives to address fear on the spiritual and perhaps the emotional plane—not in the psychological or physiological realms, though fear undeniably impacts both of those areas. This book is personal, not clinical. Its approach is more theological than pragmatic, addressing the deeper issues of the heart and leaving it up to the reader to apply it. With the exception of chapter 4, this book will not discuss specific fears and provide Bible verses to combat them. Instead, the purpose is to consider, as we wrestle with fears of any description, how the truths of God's word can comfort our questioning souls. I hope some of you will read this book in community with others so that through discussion and listening to the stories of one another, whatever help you glean from this book may be magnified.

Each chapter examines a different aspect of the struggle with fear, building on ideas in previous chapters. Chapters 1 and 2 are about the prevalence of fear and how, unlike others in the world, Christians look to God in response. Chapter 3 looks at fear and sin, and chapter 4 at fear and death. Chapter 5 casts a vision for life without dread, and chapters 6–9 explore how we can live that way, in the midst of our current circumstances, by better knowing our God and his great love for us through Jesus Christ. Next, chapter 10 examines the help we are given through Scripture and prayer, and chapter 11 investigates the role we can fulfill with one another. Finally, chapter 12 is a call to Christian courage.

In Spurgeon's discourse on Psalm 20:5 ("May we shout for joy over your salvation, and in the name of our God set up our banners! May the LORD fulfill all your petitions!"), he wrote: "The times are evil at present, but so long as Jesus lives and reigns in his church we need not furl our banners in fear, but advance them with sacred courage."[2]

---

2 Spurgeon, *Treasury of David*, 1:302.

Spurgeon described *his* times as evil. He published those words in 1869! How would he characterize *our* time? If the church of 1870 needed a call to sacred courage, how much more do we?

We strive for the dread-free life because few things declare more loudly to the watching universe that our God is glorious than Christians living serenely, venturing boldly, and waiting joyfully. Now is the time to unfurl our banners, holding fast to the hope of redemption as the world darkens. As for us, our path "is like the light of dawn, which shines brighter and brighter until full day" (Prov 4:18).

Spurgeon's voluminous commentary on the Psalms includes his aggregation of interesting and helpful insights written by others. Reading these collections, I came across some commentary on Psalm 57 by John Angiers, written in the year 1647.[3] The title of his work was "An Help to Better Hearts, for Better Times." I love this phrase! I love it when people say, "The best is yet to come." Better times are coming, and we wait for them with patience, building better hearts on the best of all hopes.

That is my hope for this work also. May it be a help to better hearts, for better times. And fear not—the best is yet to come.

> May the Lord direct your hearts to the love of God and the
> steadfastness of Christ. (2 Thess 3:5)

---

3 Spurgeon, 1:483.

1

The Prevalence of Fear

> When finally I was free to sit down beside my own fire
> I felt so tired that the flesh seemed to drag at my bones.
> I slumped down in the armchair and shut my eyes. But
> my mind was a cage gnawed by formless creatures that
> jostled and fretted, worries—some real, some half-
> recognized, some unidentified and purely instinctive—
> that wouldn't let me rest.
>
> —Mary Stewart, *Nine Coaches Waiting*

It was a dark and stormy night. I was burrowing in the closet. We were preparing to move to the other side of the world, and I was pulling out clothes to pack and clothes to toss. In the midst of a mental struggle over giving away my cardigans, for which I had a Mr. Rogers–like affinity, I heard high-pitched screams coming from the darkness of my daughters' room. I raced in there, heart thumping, to find my four-year-old huddled in her bottom bunk. She was crying hard, sweaty, and shuddering.

"I had a bad dream," she cried. "It was horrible."

"Tell Mommy," I said. "What was it?"

She could hardly choke it out. I held her, praying for God's comfort. Finally, the answer came.

"Two bunnies!"

It's funny now, but at the time, I did not laugh at my daughter. Her experience brought back memories for me. As a child, I too was plagued by nightmares. I was a fearful child in general. It's family legend that I would hide under my precious blue blankie to avoid seeing horror films such as *Dumbo* (1941). I had many terrifying dreams and often spent bedtime hours in fear—feeling jumpy, lying awake because fearful eyes don't close easily. When I couldn't stand the tortures of my anxiety anymore, I would creep silently into my parents' room and lie on the floor next to their bed. I hoped they wouldn't see me and send me back to my room. I still remember how cold I was lying there, pulling my mom's old bathrobe off the end of their bed to cover up.

The worst nightmares came after I saw the film *The Hiding Place* (1975) when I was about nine. I became terrified of the Holocaust and what happened to Corrie and Betsie ten Boom (for whom I am named). Scenes from the film played over and over in my mind. I didn't want to believe people in the world could be so wicked to each other. It made me want to find a safe place to hide. Somewhere deep inside of me, I determined always to stay safe, to stay close to home, and to be sure never to let anything bad happen to me. I looked forward to a time when I would outgrow my fears, as everyone seemed to think I would.

Eventually the nightmares lessened, and I thought fear had receded in my life. By the time I was in high school, I had begun to feel a stirring, a sort of internal restlessness, when I thought about missions. I felt maybe God was leading me that way. But missionaries tend to leave home, go far away, and take all sorts of crazy risks. It sounded to me like a dangerous life, a life of hardship. But I started to make decisions in response to the stirring in my heart. It really made no sense given how afraid I was, yet I think now God led me on, despite my fear, to follow the path he had prepared for me. After high school I went on a short-term trip to Mexico. I went away to college. I went on a trip to Israel.

One such stirring when I was twenty led me to a missions conference for college students in Atlanta. There I first became conscious of how much fear I had. John Piper was preaching from Colossians 1:24 in which Paul wrote, "In my flesh I am filling up what is lacking in Christ's afflictions." Piper said there was nothing lacking in the atonement Jesus made for our sins. The atonement was full and complete. The only thing lacking was the communication of it to the world—Jesus's death needed to be lived out in the death (either the actual death or the death-to-self) of the Christian.

In that hour I saw in the Bible, for the first time, that suffering is a planned part of the Christian life. God hasn't removed suffering for all time for those who know him—yet. This life, even when we know Jesus, isn't guaranteed to be safe. That was his plan—unavoidable, inescapable, unchangeable, out of my control. I returned to my hotel room, locked the door, laid on the dirty carpet, and cried. I wasn't wanting to serve or follow Jesus. I was weak, selfish, and terrified of suffering. God was calling me to follow him, and I did not want to do it at all.

I wish I could tell you my struggle ended that day and somehow fear in my life was triumphantly defeated for all time. But it was the beginning.

When I first married my husband, I constantly worried that he would die. I thought he would not be in this world long. I felt anxious and worried about him for no apparent reason at all. If he came from work fifteen minutes late, I'd spend the last five minutes imagining police cars pulling up, a knock at the door, a man standing there saying, "Ma'am, we have some bad news for you." Alex is healthier than a horse and tougher than a rhino. The biggest risk he took in his job at the church was probably operating the microwave. It didn't matter. I would freak out if he was late—ugly freak out.

Then my husband had a few opportunities to travel and get teaching experience in Myanmar and Nigeria. I was certain he was a dead man, and all my hopes of a happy life together were about to be ashes around my feet. I went to his funeral so many times in my mind. It didn't occur to me that this was fear operating in my life. But loving him had given me even more to fear because I had more to lose.

When we had our first baby, I learned a great deal about my subconscious. In those early months of fatigue and night-time feedings, I would frequently jerk awake and frantically slap the bedcovers, hunting for the baby. I was always sure I'd fallen asleep holding her and then squashed her or dropped her on the floor. I wouldn't remember laying her in her crib. I'd suddenly punch my husband at three o'clock in the morning, "Where's the baby? WHERE'S THE BABY!"

3

He'd say calmly, "In her crib."

You mamas, have you ever done the breathing check? What makes us risk waking our finally sleeping infant just to see if he is still alive? Where does this terror come from? Some fear that our children will drown in the bath, some that every bump and lump means cancer. What did I learn about my subconscious in those early months of motherhood? My subconscious was not trusting God. Somewhere deep inside I was very, very afraid. Whatever was built deeply into my soul as a child was still with me.

I'm more than forty years old now, have four children, and live in Indonesia. If I'm honest I still see the world in terms of safety and danger, I'm still determined to avoid suffering at all costs, and I still battle with deep and oppressive anxiety. Fear pulls the strings that move my emotions, reactions, and decisions. It seems that I am not going to passively outgrow it. It is an elemental force in my life. But I know I'm not alone.

Everyone is afraid. People live at differing levels of freedom from fear, but no one is absolutely free. It may appear that some are because our responses to fear morph and look different for each person. Not only are we afraid of different things, but our awareness of fear also differs. We show fear in different ways. Fear, as a sort of underlying emotion, can disguise itself as many other emotions. Fear is what you find underneath if you drill into insecurity. Fear is sometimes the root cause of depression and often hides beneath the mantle of anger. Do you have an anger problem? The angriest people are usually scared to death. Fear twists relationships and creates overprotectiveness, possessiveness, jealousy, and an obsession with control. A substantial portion of stress is actually fear.

Not all of us would admit to being fearful. Some of us genuinely do not identify fear among our most common feelings. But probably all of us would admit, at least at times, that we experience stress, worry, or anxiety. Psychologists and psychiatrists make a distinction between worry and anxiety. Worries, the consensus seems to be, are primarily mental, referring to thoughts in our heads. They are specific concerns, often realistic or at least possible. Anxiety is different. When this term is used clinically, it usually refers to a more diffuse and generalized state of concern, a psychic tension felt in the mind but also physically in the body. Anxiety often has an unknown or less easily labeled cause.

But both states, whatever their distinctions, are human reactions to fear occurring at some level of a person's consciousness. In this book we'll be focusing on fear itself because dealing with fear at the heart level addresses the root cause of worry, anxiety, and stress. Yet as we look at Scriptures that speak to fear, keep in mind that they speak to worry and anxiety just as clearly.

So, though it may not be obvious from the outside, everyone has a place in the heart where fears dwell. Being afraid is part of the human experience. Show me a human and I'll show you a human who, at some level, is scared. It is a constant in all our personalities and a force in all our cultures.

Roland Muller, a long-time cross-cultural worker in the Arab world, has written an insightful book on the three dominant worldview paradigms across the globe. He identifies these as guilt/innocence, honor/shame, and fear/power. Muller contends: "Down through history and across the world, these three emotional reactions to sin [guilt, shame, and fear] became the three basic building blocks that exist in all cultures today. Some cultures have more of one than another, but all three are present in all cultures today."[1] Though he claims that fear/power dynamics are present in all cultures, he points out that certain cultures more consistently see the world through a fear/power lens. They "view the universe as a place filled with gods, demons, spirits,

---

1 Muller, *Honor and Shame*, 19.

ghosts, and ancestors. Man needs to live at peace with the powers around him, and often man lives in fear."[2]

If we adopt Muller's terms, most would identify the United States as a guilt/innocence culture, but I wonder if we are shifting to become more of a fear/power culture. On the morning of September 11, 2001, I was in Introduction to Education 101 when a professor burst in, interrupted the lecturer, and put a news channel on the big screen at the front of the auditorium. We all watched in stunned silence as the towers of the World Trade Center collapsed. That day eroded the illusion of safety that had been carefully nurtured in our country for so long. Our season of geopolitical dominance erroneously convinced us of our invincibility until this event suddenly called it into question.

Since then, it seems a culture of fear has been steadily growing. (Fear is so prevalent, it's an entire culture.) Fear gets politicians elected and legislation passed. It sells newspapers, and it's why we watch the news or check social media. The "news" is rarely a factual report of what is happening; rather, it's a constant assessment of threats. After I started writing this book, the COVID-19 global pandemic began. Daily news stories showed the increasing state of fear around the world. Even now we don't know what the long-term impact of the pandemic will be, but it will certainly contribute to our fears for a long time.

I have seen firsthand that the constant, controlling forces of fear are not just dominant in the culture from which I come but are present everywhere, as Muller has posited. If you travel to the absolute farthest point from where I grew up, you will find the island where I now live. It is the world's most populated island, and its 141 million people are as culturally different from midwestern Americans as it is possible to be. But fear is a powerful, elemental force in the lives of Indonesians too. Many fears of the people around me are similar to my own, and in addition, they live in fear of spirits, ghosts, demons, and the wrath of Allah.

---

2 Muller, 42.

Though the majority religion is Islam, leading to strong honor/shame dynamics, I have often heard the religious landscape of Indonesia described as "animism with a veneer of Islam." Animism is a worldview structured around fear and appeasement. Our household helper, a practicing Muslim, bound charms around the neck of her newborn infant to prevent evil spirits from making him cry. She won't answer the door to salesmen selling bamboo brooms because they might hypnotize her with evil powers and then enter the house to steal. On the island where I live, offerings are left to appease the spirits inhabiting big trees, and no one ever goes in a graveyard unless they are with a large group attending a funeral. From the midwestern United States to its antipode on the island of Java, fear is a powerful, elemental force and a universal experience—so much so that it is part of what it means to be human (at least a human after the fall).

Was there ever a human who was not scared? It makes me wonder, was Jesus Christ ever afraid? We know from the book of Hebrews that "we do not have a high priest who is unable to sympathize with our weaknesses, but one who in every respect has been tempted as we are, yet without sin" (4:15). We also know Jesus Christ was born into a culture heavily dominated by fear/power dynamics. He entered at a time when his homeland was occupied by an oppressive foreign power, and within two generations his people headed into a total war that utterly destroyed their nation. Infectious diseases and all types of physical ailments were common, and medicine was largely undeveloped. Ghosts, demons, and evil spirits were active, and people walked in fear of them.

Although the Bible is written about specific times and places, it thoroughly addresses all aspects of the human experience. It is not silent on the subject of fear. We can see this clearly from reading about Jesus Christ and his response to the culture of fear around him.

If you read Mark's Gospel with a fear/power lens, Jesus explodes onto the scene as a total game changer. From the start, John the Baptist declares, "After me comes he who is *mightier* than I" (1:7). There are so many adjectives that John could have used, but he chose to refer to Jesus's power.

When Jesus begins to teach, the first thing observed about him, what causes a stir among the people, is that he teaches with authority (1:22). This observation is barely stated when "immediately" Jesus is tested by a feared unclean spirit. He both silences it and casts it out. These two proofs of his power are what the people chatter about and what causes people to gather about him and pursue him. "And they were all amazed, so that they questioned among themselves, saying, 'What is this? A new teaching with authority! He commands even the unclean spirits, and they obey him'" (1:27).

In fear/power cultures, people align themselves with those who are powerful as a means to protect themselves from their fears. Thus, in Mark's Gospel, Jesus is immediately thronged by an ever-growing crowd. By the end of the first chapter, his disciples are telling him, "Everyone is looking for you" (1:37). And Jesus "went throughout all Galilee, preaching in their synagogues and casting out demons" (1:39).

Soon Jesus's growing popularity makes him powerful enough to vie with other prominent figures, such as the scribes and Pharisees. In chapter 2, when Jesus pronounces forgiveness on the paralytic, they essentially accuse him of claiming power that (they believe) he does not have: "Who can forgive sins but God alone?" (2:7). Jesus frames his response in terms of power and authority:

> "Which is easier, to say to the paralytic, 'Your sins
> are forgiven,' or to say, 'Rise, take up your bed and
> walk'? But that you may know that the Son of Man
> has authority on earth to forgive sins"—he said to the
> paralytic—"I say to you, rise, pick up your bed, and go
> home." (2:9–11)

Examples of fear/power dynamics in Mark's Gospel abound, but we will look at just three more examples from the ensuing chapters. In chapter 3, because they cannot deny his power, the scribes attempt to discredit Jesus by accusing him of casting out demons by Satan's power. Jesus responds that Satan cannot cast out Satan because a divided house cannot stand. He says, "No one can enter a strong man's house and plunder his goods, unless he first binds the strong man" (3:27). In other words, a powerful figure is only bested by a more powerful figure.

Another well-known example comes from chapter 4, in which Jesus calms the storm. We know that the disciples are so thoroughly in the grip of fear that they take their imminent death as a fact: "Teacher, do you not care that we are perishing?" (4:38). Jesus arises, rebukes the wind, and says to the sea, "Peace! Be still!" And "there was a great calm" (4:39). As I once heard British theologian Vaughan Roberts say in a sermon, "Jesus speaks to the storm as if it were a naughty puppy."

In response to the disciples' panic, Jesus has demonstrated his power. Then something interesting happens: "And they were filled with great fear and said to one another, 'Who then is this, that even the wind and the sea obey him?'" (4:41). Keep in mind that this happens *after* the storm has ceased and great calm has descended. Their reaction is unexpected; they are not rejoicing, relaxing, or even sighing in relief. They are terrified. This makes sense within a fear/power cultural dynamic: the disciples have transferred their fear—to Jesus.

Note that the same reaction occurs when Jesus casts out the legion of demons who enter the pigs:

> The herdsmen fled and told it in the city and in the
> country. And people came to see what it was that
> had happened. And they came to Jesus and saw the
> demon-possessed man, the one who had had the
> legion, sitting there clothed and in his right mind, and
> they were afraid. (5:14–15)

Once the creepy, violent, naked guy is calm, dressed, and normal, *then* they become afraid. This only makes sense because they have transferred their fear to the more powerful figure.

A third appearance of the fear/power worldview follows not long after, when Jesus walks on water in chapter 6. The disciples are on the sea and the wind is against them. He comes to them, walking on the sea and, thinking he is a ghost, they are terrified (6:49). They recognize the appearance of a power far greater than themselves. When Jesus appears to them in this way, he represents a phenomenon that cannot be explained by their previous experience. Of course, they are greatly afraid.

Jesus recognizes and understands their fear. He does not scold, rebuke, or mock them. His response is compassionate and utterly reassuring: "But immediately he spoke to them and said, 'Take heart, it is I. Do not be afraid.' And he got into the boat with them, and the wind ceased" (6:50–51).

From Mark 3 and 4, we may glean two useful things to know about fear: a powerful figure (or force) can only be defeated by a more powerful one and the most powerful figure is the one to fear. From chapter 6, we see that the disciples are utterly terrified when Jesus strides on the scene and three things happen: First, he encourages them by identifying himself: "Take heart, it is I. Do not be afraid." Second, he gets into the boat with them; his immediate presence is with them where they are. And the third thing that happens? The winds ceased ... peace.

After Jesus calms the storm in chapter 4, the disciples ask, "Who then is this, that even the wind and the sea obey him?" We too should be asking this as our fears bellow and bluster around us. In the second storm, narrated in chapter 6, the same question is implied. He answers it before they can ask: "Take heart, it is I." If we are going to gain victory over our fears, if we want to be able to step forward in obedience in spite of them, then we must also ask, "Who is Jesus?" And we need to listen for his gentle reply: "Take heart, it is I." If we really grasp who he is and understand his love for us, fear loses its power, even before the storms cease.

The Bible presents a God who tenderly loves us. Jesus doesn't stand over us, finger wagging, scolding us for our weak faith when we're scared. Nor does he leave us cowering in the bottom of a beleaguered boat while he waits ashore for the storm to blow over. No, Jesus walks straight to us, sovereign over all the sound and fury. He makes himself known to us and a peace descends that, from the boat, didn't even seem possible. This is the significance of the incarnation and its beauty: Jesus came to us. He stepped into our boat. He climbed into human skin. He became, as it were, a dot on the map of our world so that he could face our dangers and feel our emotions and have his beard blasted by the winds of our storms.

Parents do not usually rebuke their children when they are afraid, no matter how silly some of their fears may seem. When my daughter had the terrifying nightmare involving two bunnies, I went to her and put my arms around her. Can we believe that our God desires to do the same, to draw near to us in our fears?

In the chapters that follow we will seek to establish that we cannot make fear dissipate completely or go away in this life. Yet what we can do is look to our God for the courage and comfort needed to face life on earth. We'll see from the Bible that God's response to fear is not condemnation. His work in us can bring us to a place where we see fear as an opportunity to hold on to him—and stand confidently in the storm.

Discussion Questions

1. What were you afraid of as a child?

2. How have these fears shaped you? What have you "built into your soul" in response?

3. What fear/power dynamics can you see in the culture(s) in which you live?

4. What fear would you most like Jesus to silence in your own life?

2

Looking beyond Fear's Anatomy

> A very young Fox, who had never before seen a Lion, happened to meet one in the forest. A single look was enough to send the Fox off at top speed for the nearest hiding place. The second time the Fox saw the Lion he stopped behind a tree to look at him a moment before slinking away. But the third time, the Fox went boldly up to the Lion and, without turning a hair, said, "Hello, there, old top."   —Aesop

If it hadn't been New Year's Day, I may not have done it. The first day of a new calendar year is just the day after December 31, yet somehow it inspires us with irresistible urges toward self-betterment. Suddenly we feel empowered to progress and develop in ways we were unable to contemplate just days before. We join gyms, make reading lists, fast from social media, and tackle the basement. One year, in the aftermath of recent catastrophe and trauma in my personal life, I felt compelled to face my fears. It was my only resolution.

We had been staying with my parents near an insect zoo called the Butterfly Pavilion. The innocent beauty of this name is utterly misleading, by the way. To me, even in January, this appellation conjured a vision of a sun-dappled structure with delicate, colorful beings fluttering about. No. I saw cockroaches, crickets, worms, wasps, and beetles in this sanctum. It is also home to approximately 120 Chilean rose-hair tarantulas, including a leggy, hairy specimen the size of your palm named "Rosie." (I am so glad now that we did not name a child that. We nearly did.)

Visitors may, for no additional charge, *hold* Rosie. It is the type of exhibit that I would ordinarily rush past with averted eyes while distracting the children with lollipops. I've always had a genuine fear of spiders, but when I was presented with this large, creepy, pinkish opportunity, it flashed into my mind that, since fear was now looming large in my life once again—deep-seated, paralyzing fear that I couldn't escape or distract myself from—perhaps the best thing to do would be to grasp it in all its hairy nastiness and have done with it. It would be a symbolic action, I told myself, a throwing down of the gauntlet in my battle with fear.

Rosie was in the care of a sweet, white-haired woman volunteer. I gingerly seated myself beside her while my husband, parents, and children, all of whom are aware of my sentiments regarding arachnids, stared.

"Now, I can tell that you are afraid," she quavered, gently placing Rosie's heavy, tickly body on my shaking palm. "So let me just tell you a little bit about Rosie's amazing anatomy. This is where she injects venom into her victims, and here is where she can shoot little hairs and bristles to infect the faces of her enemies with a nasty itchy rash. See how she's standing up a little off your hand? She's lifting up a bit because your hand is cold."

Then she said reproachfully, "You're making her nervous."

Believe me, it was mutual. As Rosie inched her way across my hand, she said, "Now that you really understand her, you won't be afraid anymore."

Wanna bet?

When the creature began to show interest in relocating to my upper arm, the lady finally reclaimed it. Before I stopped shaking long enough to stand up, she grabbed my hand and set Rosie on it again!

"The first time was because you were afraid, dear," she said. "This one's just for fun."

That's the kind of fun I had to kick off 2019. I am proud to say that both Rosie and I survived the encounter, and I was left to ponder the lady's interesting theory about fear. She thought if I knew more about the spider, if I really understood it, I wouldn't fear it. We encounter this idea constantly: if we really break down and examine our fears, if we really understand their "anatomy," we won't be afraid anymore.

This idea isn't new. In the first century AD, Plutarch wrote in his biography of Gaius Marius, a notable Roman commander, that he encouraged his soldiers to "have a good look at the enemy" as their tents were lined up for battle. "His view was that when a thing is strange it will seem more frightening even than it is, but that when one has got used to something, even something really formidable, it will cease to inspire terror."[1] This idea is everywhere. Herman Melville stated it when he wrote in *Moby Dick*, "Ignorance is the parent of fear." The thought is that all we need is more information about the things we fear.

This idea underpins much of the current approach to phobias and trauma counseling. Jordan B. Peterson, a Canadian clinical psychologist of some renown, stated in a lecture, "The alternative [to living in fear] is, let's take apart the things you're afraid of. Let's expose you to them carefully and programmatically, and then you'll learn that you're actually tougher than you think. You never knew that!"[2]

In this lecture Peterson used the example of someone who is afraid of an elevator. He claimed that repeatedly approaching an elevator is an effective clinical step. However, as he stated in the same lecture, the fear of elevators often emerges from the fear of death and repeatedly approaching it won't eliminate its threat. Perhaps by repeatedly approaching an elevator, declared Peterson, "You've learned that you can withstand the threat of death." (But you haven't. You've withstood the threat of the elevator.)

This approach assumes that fear is irrational and that an unemotional analysis of it will dismantle its threats in the cold light of reason and, perhaps, likelihood. When I was a child, plagued by nightmares of the Holocaust, people would say things like, "Don't worry—that would never happen *here*." Do you hear what this statement is saying? It invites me to hang my trust on America. As a wise old British lady said to me once, "To an American, any place outside America seems unsafe, doesn't it?"

---

1 Plutarch, *Fall of the Roman Republic*, 28.

2 Peterson, "Maps of Meaning 11."

Some trust in chariots and some trust in horses and some trust in the stars and stripes.

When we fear plane crashes or diseases, do we try to take comfort in thinking, "That almost never happens"? Are we trusting in statistics? Do we seek comfort (or to comfort others) with probabilities and likelihoods? In the end, as any of my fellow fearful people will tell you, it not comforting at all because what if I am in the less-than-one percent of cases?

It is true that fear can often amplify reality—the experience of fear ends up being worse than the actual thing we fear. As Shakespeare wrote, "A coward dies a thousand times before his death, but the valiant taste of death but once."[3] Our emotions can amplify fear, but defeating fear isn't always a matter of controlling or managing our emotions. Not all of our fears may be rational or likely, but I still find it completely inadequate merely to say so.

Perhaps the idea that taking a closer look will ease our fears comes in part from the fact that the things that children fear can seem silly and unrealistic to us. Even the fears of other adults we can sometimes dismiss as irrational and unlikely. But have we stopped to peek under the particular concern to see what they are really fearing? An actual green, warty bogeyman may not exist, but there are beings of unspeakable evil that do threaten our children.

Even in reading that, did you feel a frisson of fear because you know it's true? Children's fears are not silly. They are afraid of the same things that we are underneath: loss, loneliness, suffering, pain, death. As I have heard said by Danny Gardner, a pastor in Colorado, "Actually no one is afraid of heights. We're afraid of landing after the fall from them."

Do we see harsh realities around us? "Do we feel the world is broken? *We do.* Do we feel the shadows deepen? *We do.*"[4] Undeniably, life on earth means a fearsome array of threats of all kinds. There is enough scare power in the word *cancer* alone to make my point. You and I, living in the world we live in, must be either scared, senseless, or lying.

---

3 Shakespeare, *Julius Caesar*, 2.2.

4 Peterson, "Is He Worthy."

Because fear is not irrational. It is not silly, childish, or ridiculous. As Franklin Delano Roosevelt said in his first inaugural address in 1933: "The only thing we have to fear is fear itself—nameless, unreasoning, unjustified terror which paralyzes needed efforts to convert retreat into advance." With respect to President Roosevelt, he was wrong: we have much more to fear than just our fear. Though we can agree it is paralyzing, terror is rarely unreasonable or unjustified in the world in which we live. I would argue fear is the most rational, natural, and legitimate posture possible for a human being existing in this particular universe. We realize this long before we're big enough to spit out the toothpaste. Simply put, there *is* a Big Bad Wolf, and every child knows it. The world is not safe.

Of what are we afraid? Speaking for myself, I'm afraid of loss. I'm afraid of suffering, grief, death, and pain. I'm afraid of disability and mental illness. I'm afraid of depression. I'm afraid of not counting, not mattering, not accomplishing anything, and being a failure. I'm afraid of embarrassment and exposure. I'm afraid I'm a fake. I'm afraid of my sin, and I'm afraid of my feelings. I'm afraid I'm not good enough. I'm afraid that I'm not a good cross-cultural worker nor a good ministry wife. I'm afraid I will mess up my children; I'm afraid I already have. I'm afraid of loneliness, and I'm afraid of crowds. I'm afraid of my life not turning out like I want it to. At the bottom, underneath it all, I'm afraid I'm not loved. Also, really deep water, confined spaces, heights, and spiders. Those are just the ones I'm okay sharing with you, and I haven't listed my fears for others. As I wrote in the previous chapter, getting married and having four children quintupled my fears.

Examining our fears as a strategy for lessening them is not only a problem because it doesn't work in the end; it's also a problem because it lowers our gaze. When we analyze our fears, we focus on fear, and in the battle with fear, *what we are looking at* is key.

Sacred Courage

In college, my arachnophobia was known among my friends and sometimes resulted in a bit of teasing. One Saturday a group of us were painting the exterior of our pastor's house, an activity that brought us in contact with a fair number of spiders of various sizes and corpulencies. A Cute Nerdy Boy, the type I always went for, was teasing me about being afraid of spiders. I argued that everyone has a fear of spiders at some level—one may not mind a spider touching one's hand, but no one wants a spider in their mouth, for example.

He laughed and boasted this would not faze him. "Really?" I said. "Okay, why don't you eat one, then?"

"Sure, I would."

"Yeah, right. When you eat one, I will."

It is a truth universally acknowledged that a single man in possession of all his faculties must not want to eat a spider.[5] Right?

He promptly grabbed a big spider, tossed it in his mouth, showed it to me on his tongue, and ate it.

I cannot describe the agony of that moment. (Talk about honor/shame dynamics.) I'd given my *word*. It now seemed a very, very stupid word—but I'd given it. He offered me my choice of the remaining spiders under the eaves of the house. I just could not do it. I returned to my dorm that day with the unfulfilled promise hanging over my head like the sword of Damocles.

Not long after I returned, Cute Nerdy Boy called my room and asked me to meet him in the lounge. Still embarrassed, I did. He was there, with a paper cup containing several choice specimens of the arachnid family. The boy promptly offered the cup, generously letting me select my own victim. He seemed to think I would feel better if I kept my word, thereby preserving my self-respect.

I looked into the cup. Its paper walls were pullulating with the black threads of their legs and the dreaded fat figure-eight-shaped bodies. I started to shake. All I could see was their ugliness, their odd invertebrate

---

5 Austen, *Pride and Prejudice*, 5. This is my adaptation of her opening line.

flexibility, their swarming arthropodic horror. I could not look away. But proceeding was unthinkable.

I wanted to pass the whole thing off with humor somehow, regain some little vestige of dignity, and preserve the fragile new relationship with Cute Nerdy Boy. He was beginning to feel a little foolish, and I could tell. I guess trying to convince a girl to eat a spider isn't all it's cracked up to be. But there was no saving the situation and soon he left. Awkwardly.

That night I couldn't sleep. I'd said I would eat it if he did, and he did and I didn't. But how could I? How do I get myself into these situations? I was squarely on the horns of an ethical dilemma—or in its web.

These are the moments that define us.

The next afternoon I called him and told him I was ready. We took a walk together, back to the pastor's house, and he found me a nice specimen crawling along the shed. I had learned from my experience the day before and didn't look at it even once. I still don't know exactly what size it was, and I don't want to know. I stared straight into his beautiful blue eyes, thought about how I couldn't bear to have him think I was a coward and opened my mouth. He threw in the spider, and I swallowed hard. There was still some left, so I swallowed again. It was done.

Reader, I married him.[6]

You see it's a matter of our *gaze*. Taking a closer look at our fears neither dismantles them nor infuses our hearts with courage. As we look closer, not only are our fears still there, but we can suddenly see the ominous little hairs sprouting from their eight black legs. Spend no time studying the anatomy of your fears. Let not your encouragement to a frightened child (or your frightened self) consist of "that's impossible" (or "unlikely" or "irrational"). It isn't really, and the child knows that as well as you do. We must look elsewhere.

What do we look at?

I've argued above that fear is the most legitimate posture possible for any human being living in this particular universe. But the whole

---

6 Bronte, *Jane Eyre*, 458.

statement should be that fear is the most legitimate posture possible for any human being before we factor in God.

Apart from God we innately know, at least subconsciously, the truth about ourselves and our position in this universe. What we do not innately know—and do not innately believe—is the truth about God. Our lives without God are a journey of continual self-deceit as we endeavor to convince ourselves either that (a) we are not terrified or (b) there is nothing to be afraid of. But neither is true. The truth is we are afraid and much of our fear is legitimate. If we want to live honestly—and if we want help with our fear problem—perhaps we must start by taking a candid look at our undisguised selves, but from there we must look to God. If our gaze is focused on God, fear loses its power.

Almost four hundred years ago Thomas Fuller wrote, "Always look upwards unto a gracious God to keep thy soul steady; for looking downwards on thyself thou shalt find nothing but what will increase thy fear.... It is not thy faith, but God's faithfulness thou must rely upon."[7] So for steadiness of soul, as Fuller called it, our starting position and our continual discipline must be looking upward to God. To do this, a good place to begin is with Psalm 121, which was written, I am convinced, with the fearful in mind.

> I lift up my eyes to the hills.
>> From where does my help come?
> My help comes from the LORD,
>> who made heaven and earth.
>
> He will not let your foot be moved;
>> he who keeps you will not slumber.

---

7 Fuller, *Cause and Cure*, as quoted by Spurgeon, *Treasury of David*, 3:17–18.

Behold, he who keeps Israel
    will neither slumber nor sleep.

The LORD is your keeper;
    the LORD is your shade on your right hand.

The sun shall not strike you by day,
    nor the moon by night.

The LORD will keep you from all evil;
    he will keep your life.

The LORD will keep
    your going out and your coming in
    from this time forth and forevermore.

There is some debate about whether this psalm was written for pilgrims journeying to Jerusalem (it is one of the Psalms of Ascent, written for this type of pilgrimage) or for soldiers on the march. Either one is relevant to us because we are both pilgrims and soldiers. What we can ascertain from the text is that Psalm 121 is for those facing a daunting or dangerous undertaking and in need of help. Thus, it is even more evidently written for us because I find "facing a daunting or dangerous undertaking" an apt description of life on earth.

Our pilgrim, in need of help, looks up to the hills or the mountains. We feel his smallness, his insignificance in comparison. Confronted by their jagged, intimidating grandeur—or danger—he comforts himself that their existence points to the presence of a vast Creator, with utter sovereignty and supremacy over any possible threat. He asserts in verse 2 that the one who helps him is the one who made those mountains. As the British nature writer Robert Macfarlane wrote, "At bottom, mountains, like all wilderness, challenge our complacent conviction—so easy to lapse into—that the world has been made for humans by humans."[8] The vastness and height of the mountains broaden his perspective.

---

8 Macfarlane, *Mountains of the Mind*, 274.

21

One of the things I love about Psalm 121 is that it is so deeply relatable. Since the earliest Hebrew manuscripts did not have punctuation, the first two lines could actually be either a question or a statement: "I lift up my eyes to the hills. From where does my help come?" Or "I lift up my eyes to the hills, where my help comes from" (vv. 1–2). For me, it has been both—at times I have lifted my eyes to the hills because I know from where my help comes. I have also lifted my eyes to the hills wondering from where my help could possibly come. At the moment, is verse 1 a statement or a question for you?

In verse 3 an interesting pivot occurs. Our pilgrim has been speaking in the first person, and suddenly there's either a voice speaking to him or he begins speaking in the second person—to his audience, to us. He claims, "He will not let your foot be moved; he who keeps you will not slumber. Behold, he who keeps Israel will neither slumber nor sleep" (vv. 3–4). The word *keep*, which first appears here, occurs six times in various forms in this song. "Keep" is the Hebrew word *shamar*, which is also often translated as "watch." We are being watched over. The Lord who created the mountains in verse 2 is the one who ensures we don't slip on the heights and watches through the night when we make camp. God, in fact, is our Night Watchman.

What is the main job of a night watchman (besides watching)? He must stay awake. It is amazing how often in literature the night watchman falls asleep on duty. It's an archetype: we have the wise old man, the damsel in distress, the watchman who slumbers. In Shakespeare's *Much Ado about Nothing*, the watchmen are comic characters. Their bumbling efforts at training a new member of the watch culminate in this ironic statement from a watchman: "We will rather sleep than talk. We know what belongs to a watch."[9]

Perhaps a night watchman isn't something familiar. In many places, it is no longer a practice to set a guard through the hours of darkness. But in Southeast Asia where I live, it is common. People live in

---

9 Shakespeare, *Much Ado about Nothing*, 3.3.

organized neighborhoods, each led by a local man who functions like a village headman. In many neighborhoods, such as ours, this man selects trusted men for the night watch. Each pair takes one night a week to stay up and roam around the neighborhood between 11 p.m. and 3 a.m., checking that all is well and keeping a keen eye out for trouble. They often clang a rock on the metal gates in front of each home each time they pass, to announce they're on the watch, and to make sure no one could suspect them of sleeping on duty.

No one has too much confidence in a sleeping watchman. So we are reassured by the psalmist that this could never happen with God. This Watchman doesn't slumber, he doesn't sleep. Two terms, two ways of saying it are given for emphasis in verses 3 and 4: the idea is he doesn't nap, snooze, snore, doze, or drowse. As Eugene Peterson wrote in his paraphrase *The Message*, "Your Guardian God won't fall asleep" (v. 3).

This is what distinguishes Israel's God from idols. Idols in the ancient world were *needy*. They had to be fed and cared for. As John Walton explains, "The gods had their needs met through the temple and their images were resident in its midst, and the people had their needs met by the beneficence of the contented deity."[10]

The prophet Elijah highlights this when he confronts the prophets of Baal in 1 Kings 18. The prophets of Baal have accepted Elijah's challenge to call upon the name of their god to ignite a sacrifice, and they have called "from morning until noon" without results (v. 26). So Elijah calls to them, "Cry aloud, for he is a god. Either he is musing, or he is relieving himself, or he is on a journey, or perhaps he is asleep and must be awakened" (v. 27).

The prophet Habakkuk wrote this of idols: "Of what value is an idol carved by a craftsman? Or an image that teaches lies? For the one who makes it trusts in his own creation; he makes idols that cannot speak" (2:18 NIV). Self-help is a contradiction in terms. There is a significant difference between the help of our own creation and help from the

---

10 Walton, *Ancient Near Eastern Thought*, 90. See the entire discussion on 90–96.

Creator of all things. This is the point of Psalm 121:2 describing the Lord as the one "who made heaven and earth." We didn't make him; he made us. He's the Hill-Maker and the Wakeful Watchman. He is our keeper, taking up his umbrella-like protective stance right beside us. In the psalmist's words, he "is your shade on your right hand" (121:5).

The writer promises in verse 6 that "the sun shall not strike you by day nor the moon by night." We have the sun and the moon, the day and the night: two pairs of opposites. There is another pair in verse 8: "The LORD will keep your going out and your coming in from this time forth and forevermore." Opposites can be used as a way of implying that not only are the extremes covered but also everything in between. We can see this clearly from the use of alpha and omega, the first and last letters in the Greek alphabet, in Revelation 1:8. "'I am the Alpha and the Omega,' says the Lord God, 'who is and who was and who is to come, the Almighty.'" He isn't just the A—the beginning—and the Z—the end—he is every letter in between. So in Psalm 121 when we hear that our Watchman protects us under sun and moon, day and night, going out and coming in, now and forever, we are meant to hear this as *universal uninterrupted coverage.*

Psalm 121 tells us where to look when fear casts its dark shadow over us. We look to God, who is surely on duty. As we begin to address our fears, let's ask ourselves where we're hanging our trust. Let's agree not to deal with fear by analyzing it so that we can reassure ourselves that the events we fear could not or are not likely to happen.

The real help is in the Mountain-Maker, the Wakeful Watchman who is on duty all the time. Fighting fear begins, not by taking a closer look at our fears, but by taking a closer look at the One who is on our side. As Corrie ten Boom put it, "If you look at the world, you'll be distressed. If you look within, you'll be depressed. But if you look at Christ, you'll be at rest."[11]

---

11 Corrie ten Boom, *The Hiding Place.*

Discussion Questions

1. What advice have you heard from the world about fighting fear? Have you followed it? How did it work out?

2. In what situations have you been inclined to comfort yourself with reasoning or statistics?

3. What verses in Psalm 121 are most comforting to you?

4. What would it look like to gaze at God in your fear? How would you do that?

3

Is Fear a Sin?

> Nevermind if the trouble shews no sign of giving way: it is just when it seems most hopelessly unyielding, holding on through the spring days, alive and strong, it is then that the tiny buds appear that soon will clothe it with glory. Take the very hardest thing in your life—the place of difficulty, outward or inward, and expect God to triumph gloriously in that very spot. Just there He can bring your soul into blossom!   —Lilias Trotter, *Parables of the Cross*

My dad and the dog were up, but the sun was not. We were sitting in the armchairs in the family room, drinking coffee and enjoying the peace of early morning. I loved those times with my dad when we could just talk, uninterrupted, about whatever we liked.

"I was reading that Spurgeon book," he said. "He wrote something in there that really helped me. He was writing about trials, and it made me realize that this thing I'm going through is just a trial."

The thing he was going through was his recent diagnosis, at sixty-five, with Alzheimer's disease. It wasn't a small thing. He was already beginning to experience difficulty doing many things and having to adjust daily, even hourly, to what was happening in his brain.

I stared at him, thinking, Of course it's a trial. It's probably one of the worst things to ever happen to either of us; if it isn't a trial then what is it? But then I realized what he was saying. It was so difficult, in the aftermath of diagnosis, to know what to do with it—how to respond. Recognizing his illness as a trial helped him tremendously. He may not have known what to do about Alzheimer's, but a lifetime of following Jesus had taught him what to do about trials.

"I realized it changes nothing," he said, smiling at me. "God loves me, and God plans my life. Trials come, and I will walk through them with him."

That conversation was a few years ago already, but I remember it so often it could be yesterday. My dad showed me the significance of putting things in their proper categories. Alzheimer's isn't something new, strange, random, or unplanned. It's a trial and thus an opportunity to trust God and take comfort in him. When we think rightly about the nature of the things we face, we can see the opportunities they present.

My dad's insight into his own situation prompts an important question we must consider as we struggle with fear: To what category does it belong? Is it a sin? (Ask that one in a room full of people and prepare for liftoff.) What opportunity does fear present? Does it call for repentance? For prayer? As my dad's experience shows, defining what the struggle actually is helps us know how to respond.

There are so many reasons to put fear in the sin category. For one, fear is a result of the fall. Fear and sin were born together in the garden. Before Eve and Adam transgressed against God, they had nothing to fear. In the first chapter, I referred to Roland Muller's work on the three main worldview paradigms: guilt/innocence, honor/shame, and power/fear. Muller states that these three paradigms are rooted in what happened in the garden of Eden when Adam and Eve disobeyed God. He identifies guilt, shame, and fear as human emotional responses to sin. The first mention of fear in the Bible occurs in Genesis 3 after Adam and Eve ate the forbidden fruit.

> And they heard the sound of the LORD God walking
> in the garden in the cool of the day, and the man
> and his wife hid themselves from the presence of the
> LORD God among the trees of the garden. But the
> LORD God called to the man and said to him, "Where
> are you?" And he said, "I heard the sound of you in
> the garden, and I was afraid, because I was naked, and
> I hid myself." (3:8–10)

Is Fear a Sin?

The change in Adam's circumstances is incredible. By one act of disobedience his awareness, his relationships, and his security have been utterly transmogrified. He dares not face God again; he runs for cover in the trees. Imagine him threading desperately through paradise, blind to its beauty, now seeing it only as providing a place to hide. God's presence is now even more dangerous than his absence. We can see, as far back as the garden, that fear has its roots in sin. In short, fear exists because sin does. It comes with our current human state and is a deeply entwined part of our spiritual DNA after the fall.

A second reason why fear is often judged to be sin is that Scripture forbids us to fear. This is probably the reason we hear the most often. The Bible's pronouncements against fear cannot be mistranslations, copy errors, or grammatical misunderstandings because they occur repeatedly in different words in books of different biblical genres. It was said by Moses, Joshua, Elisha, Isaiah, Jesus, John, Peter, and Paul.[1] It is commonly said that the Bible tells us not to fear at least once for every day of the year. The exact number is hard to calculate, but the message is clear: God does not want his people to be afraid. "Do not fear" is said in the same grammatical construction as "Do not commit adultery" and "Do not kill."

A third reason some consider fear sinful is because it often causes us to distrust God. Paul Tripp wrote, "For the believer, fear is always God-forgetful. If God is sovereign and his rule is complete, wise, righteous, and good, why would you fear?"[2] Fear readily roots in the distrustful soil of our hearts. It is for the *unbeliever* that fear is the most legitimate and reasonable posture possible, living in this universe. For the believer in the God of the Bible, fear tempts us to refuse to trust in the sovereign will and providence of our good God. As Henry Melvill pointed out,

---

1 Moses (Exod 14:13; Deut 3:22; 7:18; 20:1); Joshua (Josh 10:25; 11:6); Elisha (2 Kgs 6:16); Isaiah (Isa 8:12–13; 41:13–14); Jesus (Matt 14:27; 17:6–7); Peter (1 Pet 3:6, 14); and Paul (2 Tim 1:7). There are more examples of each.

2 Tripp, *New Morning Mercies*, 9.

You cannot distrust God, and not accuse him of a
want either of power or of goodness; you cannot
repine—no, not even in thought—without virtually
telling him that his plans are not the best, nor his
dispensations the wisest, which might have been
appointed in respect of yourselves.[3]

As we will see in chapter 8, fear leads the believer straight into a struggle with the will of God. In every arena of our lives, in every new form, it begs the question: Are we going to trust Him?

A final reason why many classify fear as a sin is because it can keep us from obedience. Consider the Israelite spies at Canaan in Numbers 13. The great exodus of God's people from Egypt has occurred, the people of Israel have made it through the wilderness to the promised land, and they find it inhabited already by many fierce peoples who have no intention of peacefully vacating. Spies are sent by Moses, and they return after forty days and report that the land "flows with milk and honey, and this is its fruit. However, the people who dwell in the land are strong, and the cities are fortified and very large. And besides, we saw the descendants of Anak there" (vv. 27–28).

Caleb encourages the people, evidently responding in panic, to be still. He urges Moses to invade at once, "for we are well able to overcome it" (v. 30). But the other spies reiterate their "bad report" (v. 32), rapidly ballooning it with hyperbole:

The land ... is a land that devours its inhabitants, and
all the people that we saw in it are of a great height.
And there we saw the Nephilim (the sons of Anak,
who come from the Nephilim), and we seemed to
ourselves like grasshoppers, and so we seemed to
them. (vv. 32–33)

3 Henry Melvill on Psalm 78:18, as quoted by Spurgeon, *Treasury of David*, 1:354.

By this report, they are not going to consume the milk and honey of the land—the land is going to consume them. Every single human in it, they claim, is a giant of such huge proportions that the warriors of Israel are like leggy little insects.

How does the congregation respond? See how readily they slide into disobeying God's command to march in and possess the land. They call out in panic, cry all night, complain about their leadership, and doubt the Lord (14:1–4). (This progression is, sadly, only too familiar to me.) When Joshua and Caleb urge them not to fear but to trust God's protection, they prepare to stone them. Only the glory of the Lord appearing at the tent of meeting stops them. God's response makes it clear that they are in sin:

> How long will this people despise me? And how long
> will they not believe in me, in spite of all the signs that
> I have done among them? I will strike them with the
> pestilence and disinherit them, and I will make of you
> a nation greater and mightier than they. (14:11–12)

The main reasons that some want to put fear in the sin category are because fear and sin began together in the garden, Scripture forbids us to fear, and fear leads us into distrust and disobedience. So is fear itself a sin? If not a sin of commission, is it a sin of omission—a lack of faith? How does *God* view it? Are we sinning when we feel afraid?

Let's take another look at the story of the Israelite spies. In Christian discussions of fear, this story is often used to support the idea that fear is sinful. And yet, from what I can see, God did not punish the people of Israel because the spies' report made them fearful. He became angry and punished them because of the way they *responded* to that fear. Ask yourself, what would have happened if the people had responded to that scary report by falling to their knees and asking God to help and guide them? Or perhaps by shouting in anticipation as they awaited God's victory? "I can't wait to see how God will defeat the giant scary humans!" That was not what they did. They instantly began to panic, to grumble, and to question God. They even decided they were ready to abandon God's leadership and protection and return to a state of slavery! "'Why is the LORD bringing us into this land, to fall by the sword? Our wives and our little ones will become a prey. Would it not be better for us to go back to Egypt?' And they said to one another, 'Let us choose a leader and go back to Egypt'" (14:3–4).

God judged them for despising him and for unbelief. We can see the strong thread of fear throughout this passage, but there were worse things afoot. The idea that their crimes go beyond merely being afraid is reinforced when God pronounced a punishment on the people:

> None of the men who have seen my glory and my
> signs that I did in Egypt and in the wilderness, and yet
> have put me to the test these ten times and have not
> obeyed my voice, shall see the land that I swore to give
> to their fathers. And none of those who despised me
> shall see it. (14:22–23)

God names their transgressions: they have tested him, disobeyed him, and despised him.[4] But he doesn't mention fear—only the actions they took in *response* to it.

Someone said to me once, "We tend to be compassionate with the fearful. But God is angry." Is he? Is it anger that says, "Do not be afraid, little flock, for your Father has chosen gladly to give you the kingdom" (Luke 12:32 NIV)? It seems to me that God is gentle with the fearful, not condemning. When our *reactions* to fear are distrust and disobedience, then his judgment justly falls.

---

4 They "have put me to the test these ten times" (Num 14:22)—just as there were ten plagues before Pharoah obeyed in Exodus 7–12. In this instance they are no better than Pharoah!

Is Fear a Sin?

It is helpful to think of fear's relationship with sin in the same way that we think of anger's relationship with sin. Not all anger is sin, but the two lie closely together. Anger thrusts us into sin almost before we know it and trying to unravel righteous emotions or motives from our anger is difficult, the more so because we cannot see our own hearts, emotions, and reactions clearly. But we would say that some anger is clearly not sin, such as the righteous wrath evinced at times by Jesus.

When the desert fathers identified the seven deadly sins to be overcome in the life of the Christian, they included wrath—but defined it as hatred or a wish for vengeance.[5] Dorothy L. Sayers, in her introduction to Dante's *Purgatory*, delineates this wrath as "love of justice perverted to revenge and spite."[6] Here we see a sinful manifestation of anger, utterly different from the righteous emotion of Christ. So anger, as an emotion, can have either sinful or righteous causes and lead to either sinful or righteous actions. Perhaps we should think of fear in the same way. Just as Paul warns the Ephesians, "In your anger do not sin," so we ought to say, "In your fear do not sin."

In his famous epistolary work *The Screwtape Letters*, C. S. Lewis records Screwtape, the senior demon, instructing his apprentice Wormwood as he multiplies temptations against his Christian subject. "For remember," he writes, "the act of cowardice is all that matters; the emotion of fear is, in itself, no sin and, though we enjoy it, does us no good."[7]

Some claim that fear must be a sin because you cannot live in fear and faith at the same time. It is often said fear and faith cannot coexist; they cannot live together. But our real state is often a mixture of both at the same time. I think I've lived nearly my whole life in both. We see both in the lives of others, too. Look at David in Psalm 57. He says,

---

5 Fear does not appear on this list, which includes pride, greed, wrath, envy, lust, gluttony, and sloth.

6 Dorothy L. Sayers in the introduction to Dante's *Divine Comedy, Part 2*, 67.

7 Lewis, *Screwtape Letters*, 163.

"In you my soul takes refuge" (v. 1) and "My soul is in the midst of lions" (v. 4). He says, "My soul was bowed down" (v. 6) and "My heart is steadfast" (v. 7). Charles Spurgeon commented on this passage: "Note the varying condition *of the same heart, at the same time.*"[8] Do we see ourselves as wildly inconsistent, oscillating rapidly between fearfulness and faithfulness? If so, we're in good company.

It is interesting how passively David describes fear in Psalm 55. He writes, "Fear and trembling *come upon* me, and horror overwhelms me" (v. 5). His primary emotion here is fear. But David knows it is incumbent upon him to trust God, and he repeatedly directs his calls to the right place: "But I call to God and the LORD will save me. Evening and morning and at noon I utter my complaint and moan, and he hears my voice" (vv. 16–17). David's response to being overwhelmed by dread is a faithful one: he increases his prayers. He ends the song reaffirming his unshaken trust in God. It seems faith and fear can coexist in the righteous soul.

I conclude then that fear is an emotion; one that, like anger, powerfully tempts us to sinful responses. We cannot ignore, deny, reason away, or eradicate it from our human experience. Fear is a part of our experience in this world but won't exist in the one to come. (It isn't just our tears that will be forever wiped away, friends—our fears will be, too.) Determining whether fear is a sin is not just an exercise in splitting hairs; it yields an important insight that will help us as we struggle with it. The insight is this: Fear is an opportunity.

As we have seen, in response to it we can doubt God, complain of our weakness or circumstances, and rebel against potential plans for our lives. We can seize our desires and demand satisfaction of them. We can search for somewhere to place our trust besides God. And we can shrink back from obedience.

---

8 Spurgeon, *Treasury of David*, 1:485 (emphasis added).

Is Fear a Sin?

I have written some already about my own struggle with fear. I have often doubted God. I know that I am not entirely innocent in this, as if it is somehow not my fault and I cannot help it because the world is such a scary place. Distrust isn't something that just happens to us, arising from outside and taking us over. Distrust has often been my chosen response.

But fear also presents us with an opportunity for a different response: trusting God. It really is a call to battle. It is a rallying cry for faith to rise as we repeatedly affirm our trust in God and his sovereign plans. When fear rises, we, far from being somehow disqualified or condemned because we are afraid, can journey forward in courage with God.

We've considered David. Let's look at another biblical figure who wasn't disqualified for being afraid: Gideon in the book of Judges. Was his fear a sin? More importantly, how did God react to his fear?

Gideon is a champion to whom I can relate. I can identify with his constant need for reassurance. Gideon was living in a fearful time for the Israelites—a time when the people of Midian were violently oppressing them, pillaging their crops, and spoiling their lands (Judg 6:2-6).

Gideon is in a winepress in the offseason, using it to secretly thresh some of the wheat crop before it can be taken by the Midianites. He is in hiding, effectively in a state of fear. The angel of the Lord appears and says to him, "The LORD is with you, O mighty man of valor" (6:12). Gideon's response is laden with doubt and fear:

> If the LORD is with us, why then has all this happened
> to us? And where are all his wonderful deeds that our
> fathers recounted to us, saying, "Did not the LORD
> bring us up from Egypt?" But now the LORD has
> forsaken us and given us into the hand of Midian. (6:13)

Talk about doubting God! Again and again in the Old Testament, God establishes his character and his faithfulness to his people by citing the exodus. The act of delivering his people from bondage, bringing them through the wilderness, and leading them into the promised land is the bedrock evidence of the kind of God that he is and would be for his people. It is a central, foundational motif for their understanding of God. This is not gentle pondering on Gideon's part—this is blatant distrust in the face of fear.

The angel responds, "Go in this might of yours and save Israel from the hand of Midian; do I not send you?" (6:14). He is answering the charge that God is unfaithful by arguing that he is doing something—he has come to send Gideon. But Gideon is understandably unimpressed by this. "'Please, Lord, how can I save Israel? Behold, my clan is the weakest in Manasseh, and I am the least in my father's house.' And the LORD said to him, 'But I will be with you, and you shall strike the Midianites as one man'" (6:15–16).

The word *but* at the beginning of the Lord's response should be on a list of significant Bible conjunctions. It makes all the difference. To Gideon, however, it still isn't enough. He asks for a sign that it is actually God who is speaking to him. He then needs reassurance that the angel won't depart before he can bring out his offering! When Gideon returns with an offering of food, the angel has him soak the food with broth and then taps it with his staff. When fire springs from the rock and consumes the offering, Gideon perceives that he is the angel of the Lord and, immediately, is once again afraid (we are expecting this by now). "And Gideon said, 'Alas, O Lord GOD! For now I have seen the angel of the LORD face to face.' But the LORD said to him, 'Peace be to you. Do not fear; you shall not die'" (6:22–23).

The response to his request for a sign is pretty conclusive, so what does Gideon do? March forth in faith? No. He falls apart in fear because he has seen the angel of the Lord, needing reassurance yet again. God's first order to this fearful soldier begins at home—he is to pull down his father's idols of Baal. Gideon does so, "but because he was too afraid of his family and the men of the town to do it by day, he did it by night" (6:27).

As the story goes on, Gideon gathers an army and prepares to march on the Midianites. But "all the Midianites and the Amalekites and the people of the East came together, and they crossed the Jordan and encamped in the Valley of Jezreel" (6:33). The enemy is gathering, gaining in strength and looming nearer. In the face of these concentrated enemies, Gideon needs reassurance yet again. He tests God by laying out a dry fleece overnight, asking him to make it wet with dew but the ground around it dry. In the morning he wrings enough water out of it to fill a bowl. He is not convinced. Maybe he was wondering if there was a scientific explanation. So he reverses the rules and tests again—now he needs the fleece dry and the ground wet.

At this point, I honestly wonder why God is not done with Gideon. Don't get me wrong, Gideon's feelings make complete sense from *Gideon's perspective*. All he has is a vague calling from a visitor, albeit a supernatural one, and a horde of evil enemies waiting to destroy him. It is from *God's perspective* that this passage is shocking. He has patiently tended to Gideon, repeatedly bringing him up to scratch as Gideon wavers and worries. He clothes Gideon with his own Spirit to help him obey (v. 34) and responds to every doubt that Gideon brings to him. Why hasn't God thrown in the towel (or the fleece) and given up on Gideon? Or at least disciplined him for his fear?

What does God do? God announces that Gideon's limited forces are, in fact, too large, so that when God brings the victory they will think they did it themselves. God says, "Whoever is fearful and trembling, let him return home and hurry away from Mount Gilead" (7:3). If we needed any further evidence that this story is meant to teach us about fear, there it is. The soldiers who choose to go home in fear will not have the opportunity to see the great triumph of God. God then cuts the army yet again, with the famous "drinking like a dog" test (7:5–7).

Gideon returns to camp with just three hundred men (and the three hundred who drink with interesting manners). How do we think he feels? Here is where we see the amazing beneficence of God. For once, Gideon does not ask for a sign. But God mercifully offers it to him that night, as he is no doubt contemplating his tiny forces in terror. It is a stunning act of pure, gratuitous mercy toward fearful Gideon that utterly undoes me. God sends Gideon down to the camp of the enemy to listen to what they say. God says, "Afterward your hands shall be strengthened to go down against the camp" (7:11).

When Gideon listens in, he hears an enemy soldier relating a strange dream of a barley cake rolling into the camp and flattening a tent. His comrade replies, "This is no other than the sword of Gideon the son of Joash, a man of Israel; God has given into his hand Midian and all the camp" (7:14). Gideon worships God.

He returns to his three hundred men and they surround the enemy with trumpets and lanterns in jars. Gideon, reassured at last, instructs them to give a victory shout before the battle even begins: "For the LORD and for Gideon" (7:18). There is no discernible fear in Gideon's words or actions after God gives him that last sign—a sign graciously given on the eve of battle, for which he didn't even ask. God made provision for Gideon's fear and was ready with every bit of help and reassurance he needed.

Often, when hearing this story, many, including myself, point out all the times Gideon is afraid and needs reassurance. But what about God? He gives that reassurance over and over. He clothes Gideon with his Spirit to lead him into obedience. He is waiting on that last dark night with exactly the encouragement that Gideon needs to march on to victory with joy. Many hear the irony in the angel's initial greeting to Gideon: "The LORD is with you, O mighty man of valor" (6:12). But are we sure it is sarcastic? Is that usually God's *métier*? Or is God greeting Gideon as God sees him? Has God effectively renamed Gideon in the same way that he renamed Abram the childless as Abraham, the "father of many nations"? It is not Scripture's first seemingly ironic renaming nor its last. We hear the irony in the angel's choice of address, but I think it was said to him in all seriousness. With God on his side, Gideon is a mighty man of valor.

Gideon was afraid again and again. But he did not sin. In every situation, he kept moving forward in obedience. Gideon is even mentioned in the "Faith Hall of Fame" in Hebrews 11, listed among those who, by faith, "were made strong out of weakness, became mighty in war, put foreign armies to flight" (v. 34).

Fear is like a large, dark shadow, looming between us and the light. It casts darkness over us and our prospects. Fear would impel us to doubt and distrust God and prevent us from walking forward in faith. It constantly raises the question: Can God be trusted? If fear itself is not sin nor a step from the right path, it can still make that path appear so dark that it prompts many missteps.

That is the place where every new fear finds us: standing on the path, one foot raised for the next step. And the light dims. Is God angry now? Or is he presenting us with a new opportunity to be clothed by the Spirit and go forward in faith, as he did Gideon? It's not merely a cliché: God really does want us to "walk by faith, not by sight" (2 Cor 5:7). Fear puts us in circumstances where we must do so.

Fear may present us with powerful temptations to sin, but it simultaneously gives us opportunities to walk by faith, to tread our earthly measure clothed in Spirit-filled courage as we await the deliverance of God. Our posture, then, should be like David's in Psalm 56:3–4: "When I am afraid, I put my trust in you. In God, whose word I praise, in God I trust; I shall not be afraid. What can flesh do to me?" When David's fear arises, he responds with renewed trust.

Dear heart, let's repent not of fear but of our responses to it. And let's start seeing our fear as a call to action—a place for faith to rise. In the next chapter, we will look at the deepest and most central fear of all and how it can be used to strengthen our souls.

Sacred Courage

Discussion Questions

1. Have you ever felt guilty or ashamed for being afraid? Describe.

2. What are ways that you respond to fear? Are those responses sinful? Why or why not?

3. What is a step of obedience you need to take even though you feel afraid to do so?

4

You Shall Surely Die

Death, be not proud, though some have called thee
Mighty and dreadful, for thou art not so;
For those whom thou think'st thou dost overthrow
Die not, poor Death, nor yet canst thou kill me.
From rest and sleep, which but thy pictures be,
Much pleasure; then from thee much more must flow,
And soonest our best men with thee do go,
Rest of their bones, and soul's delivery.
Thou art slave to fate, chance, kings, and desperate men,
And dost with poison, war, and sickness dwell,
And poppy or charms can make us sleep as well,
And better than thy stroke; why swell'st thou then?
One short sleep past, we wake eternally,
And Death shall be no more; Death, thou shalt die.
—John Donne, Holy Sonnet 10

Before it happened, I would have said that I wasn't afraid to die. Not out of bravado—I truly believed it. I did not consciously feel afraid to die. If you had asked me, I would have uttered the usual Christian sentiments quite readily: "I know where I'm going." "I'm going to a better place." "Death isn't the end." As I've written, there were many realities that I feared, but I believed that death wasn't one of them.

After our first year living overseas, my husband began to travel occasionally. He was frequently invited to teach short-term modular courses for the seminary in other places around the country where we live. He would be away for a week at a time while I stayed home with the children.

Some aspects of being alone were a little challenging for me—not only being solely responsible for our four young children around the clock but dealing with other things too, like unknown people coming to the door or changing out the heavy gas tanks and water jugs that keep our home running. I always felt more vulnerable in the house at night with my husband away, even though our house in Indonesia has iron bars on all the windows, a heavy metal gate with a padlock out front, and significant locks on the front door. But I was getting better at being alone, and whenever he received an invitation to travel and teach, I would urge him to go.

In October 2018, he was invited to a city on the other side of the island to teach a one-week course. By the last night of the course, we were all eager for him to come home. I put the children to bed and puttered around doing random household chores. I repainted the bit of wall above the tiles in the bathroom and started cooking a big pot of oranges on the stove to make marmalade.

By ten o'clock I was getting tired, which was really the goal of all this activity because I never sleep well when my husband is away. I wanted the marmalade to cool a little more before I went to bed, so, seeing that the kids had left Legos all over the floor in the family room, I sat there for a bit. I was building a bat cave for Lego Batman, knowing it would keep my nearly four-year-old son busy while I homeschooled the girls in the morning. My cell phone rang, and it was my husband, finally done with his evening's teaching and ready to talk.

In the middle of our conversation, I suddenly felt heavy-duty pins and needles in my right leg. Thinking I had just been sitting on the hard tile floor too long, I started to shift my position. Then I felt a wave of body panic wash over me, sort of like the feeling you get when you are about to throw up (or give birth) and you know it's urgent. We were still on the phone and I just had time to say, "I feel strange. Something's happening ..."

The entire right side of my body utterly collapsed. I lost all feeling and ability to move and fell to the floor on my left side. I was still clutching my phone in my left hand and I could hear my husband asking, "Betsy, are you there? Is everything okay? Did you hang up?"

I tried to answer his questions, but my mouth wouldn't move. I tried to tell him I needed help, but I couldn't get any words to form. I was trapped in my own helpless body, and all I could do was pray that he wouldn't hang up.

"Are you okay? Are you there?"

I knew immediately that something serious was happening. I was fighting to stay conscious, feeling my eyes shut. I gripped the phone and concentrated with all my might on getting my mouth to move. After a minute or two of what my husband describes as gibberish, I finally managed to get out two words he understood—Call Michelle—a friend who lived nearby. Getting my mouth to move felt like leaving the dentist and accidentally chewing on my own cheek without even knowing it. My teeth feel like someone else's teeth in my mouth.

He understood enough and said he would hang up and call for help. Hearing that phone go dead while lying on the floor was the loneliest I have ever felt. I believed I was dying. All I could think of was those four little children waking up on a sunny morning and running downstairs to find my dead body on the floor. *Dear Jesus.*

I managed to type "Help" into my phone with my left hand and send it to a circle of local friends. Then it occurred to me, the house was all locked up! No one would be able to get in and help me. I was not only imprisoned helplessly in my own body but also in my own house. All of my being focused on one thing: I had to get the front door open. I bellowed my oldest daughter's name as loudly as I could, over and over. She was sleeping soundly and did not wake up. (Let me just say, I praise Jesus that she did not wake up!) I was lying about twenty feet from the front door, but the key that I needed to open it was on a nail on the back of our bedroom door, ten feet away and six feet off the ground.

I shoved my phone into my clothes and began to drag my collapsed body across the floor on my left arm. It was slow going, and at one point, I felt something holding me back. I looked around and saw my own lifeless right arm tangled on the leg of the coffee table as I passed it. I'd had no idea. By the time I made it to the bedroom door, I was able to use my right arm clumsily, some movement coming slowly back. I climbed up the doorframe with my left arm and stood on my left leg, but I couldn't let go to grab the key or I'd fall, dragged down by my own dead weight. In desperation I swung my numb right arm to bat the key off the hook. When the key fell, I did. I let go of the door, dropped to the floor, and managed to grab the key with my left hand.

By the time I'd dragged myself to the front door, my right hand was coming back. I unlocked the door and fell next to it, trying to lean my back against the wall so I wouldn't be lying on my face. Within two minutes, I heard someone arrive, climb the iron gate, and come to the door. Two minutes later, another couple came. These friends eventually drove me to a hospital in the nearest city, about an hour away. When it became clear that the hospital in our country could not help me, they brought me home again to prepare to evacuate to Singapore.

I suffered a stroke that night, caused by a blood clot that hit my left brain. As strokes go, it was minor because I recovered the use of the right side of my body quickly. I was not, as I feared during those terrible minutes, dying. But I believed I was. My *body* believed I was. And I was suddenly, blindingly terrified.

I learned that I am desperately afraid to die. I did not know that before. In the aftermath, as I went through weeks of medical testing in Singapore and an evacuation to the United States for more neurologists and tests, I found in myself a deep and forceful fear of dying that colored everything dark for a long time. The stroke shattered my illusion of safety. For the first time in my life, the specter of my own mortality loomed over me.

In the throes of PTSD, I was afraid to be alone. I was afraid of every new sensation in my weakened body. I was so afraid of another stroke. I would often wake up in the night and find half of my body completely numb because my brain was reliving what happened. I would scream repeatedly for help, but no sounds would come out because my brain was convinced I was having another stroke and couldn't produce any noise.

It was ugly and weird. I experienced chronic panic attacks, coming on without warning. Suddenly I would feel a sort of hot spasm shoot up and down my spine, I would become intensely nauseous, and it would feel like all the air I was breathing had no oxygen in it. My hearing would tunnel out or be filled with a loud ringing. It took me a while to identify these episodes as panic attacks, but that is what they were.

For a long time, I was afraid to shower. It was many months before I could be behind a locked door without starting to shake. Forcing myself to be home alone, to take a walk without my phone, to drive a car again, and to let my husband go anywhere were all huge leaps of faith for me. Each one involved a painful struggle before I could get there. After six months of medical leave in the United States, we returned to our home overseas, where good medical care is not available. It felt like facing death all over again.

Suddenly I not only saw my own fear of death, I saw it everywhere around me. It was as though clarity washed over my vision. I saw that all of humankind is living under the looming shadow of the death that is coming to us all. I began to see how thoroughly this impacts the entire human experience.

The Bible itself opens with this incredible, devastating reality. Man is beautifully, wonderfully brought into being by God himself and given a glorious world to inhabit. God requires only his obedience and, essentially, his allegiance to God his Creator. If he transgresses, God says, "You shall surely die" (Gen 2:17). We know that he does transgress. The judgment God pronounces on him is the impossible, mind-boggling verdict that he cannot continue to live. Yet he has no concept of death or experience of it. The verdict is stunning, too terrible to be true. The one thing he knows is his own existence and being, through which all of his experience of reality is filtered. Now he must live each day of it with the knowledge of its inevitable end.

Leo Tolstoy wrote about a moment of clarity like this that came suddenly to his character Konstantin Levin in *Anna Karenina*:

> Death, the inevitable end of everything, presented itself to him for the first time with irresistible force. And this death, which here, in his beloved brother, moaning in his sleep and calling by habit, without distinction, now on God, now on the devil, was not at all as far off as it had seemed to him before. It was in him, too—he felt it. If not now, then tomorrow, if not tomorrow, then in thirty years—did it make any difference? And what this inevitable death was, he not only did not know, he not only had never thought of it, but he could not and dared not think of it.
> "I work, I want to do something, and I've forgotten that everything will end, that there is—death. Yet I'm still alive. And what am I to do now, what am I to do?"[1]

Perhaps this moment of clarity comes to everyone at some point. Robert Frost famously said at his eightieth birthday celebration that he could sum up everything he had learned about life in three words: "It goes on."[2] Yet I think we all reach a place where we realize, at least in terms of the life we live, it doesn't. Frost died nine years later. We live, we die. As Spurgeon wrote, "Here is the history of the grass—sown, grown, blown, mown, gone; and the history of man is not much more."[3]

Have we come to grips with the reality of our own death? Or are we, like the wider culture around us, too busy denying it? It seems to me that American culture in particular sanitizes death and ignores it. Many have never even seen the dead body of a person; if we do, it has been painted to look lifelike.

---

1 Tolstoy, *Anna Karenina*, 348.

2 Josephs, "Robert Frost's Secret."

3 Spurgeon on Psalm 90:6; 103:15. *Treasury of David*, 2:62.

You Shall Surely Die

The first time I saw a dead body I thought there was some mistake; surely, he was just deeply asleep. I was a small child, and he had been my great-grandfather. As my family walked slowly past his coffin, I reached out my hand and touched the tip of his nose. It was hard, like thick plastic, and cold. My father scowled, and I dropped my hand back into the folds of my dress. He wouldn't be playing old show tunes on the piano and giving me vanilla ice cream in little blue and white dishes anymore. Someone else would live in the old house with the rose garden. He was gone. I didn't consciously think about death again for many years.

My family now lives in a culture where death's encroachment is harder to deny. On Java, when a person passes away, a black flag is hung at the entrance to the street and word travels quickly from house to house. The family and nearest neighbors immediately prepare the body, laying it out in a big box—under glass, if they can afford it. The glass is the only separation from the sight and smell of death. Burial must occur quickly in a hot climate such as this, so no one goes to work that day or, at the latest, the next. I have seen many grayed, dead bodies now, lying in state as the village trails past.

On the holiday of Idul Adha, Muslims slaughter goats to commemorate Abraham's offering of his son Ishmael, as they believe. On this day goats are penned in front of mosques around town, and men gather with machetes to slit their throats and lay the bodies against the gutter so their blood can drain. Bleating goats become bleeding goats in an instant. It is hard to imagine that scene in the United States. Living here has made me recognize how thoroughly Americans have managed to detach themselves from the idea of death.

Yet, however we try to cover it up, the awareness of death will not be suppressed. It is always there underneath. Consider popular mottos about life. They actually imply that death approaches. "Life is good" (so enjoy it while you have it). Live "your best life now" (because you don't have later). "You only live once" (and when it's over, it's over). Even the Latin classic *carpe diem* ("seize the day") is really followed by an invisible *tempus fugit* ("time flies").

My second chapter argued that we shouldn't examine our fears in an attempt to reason ourselves out of them or make them disappear. So why should we take a closer look at the biggest fear of them all? Think about how many of our fears are, in fact, the fear of death. The fear of death is the underlying root fear of many other fears, and I believe there is something to be gained from tackling it head-on. The fear of death can become extremely useful for the Christian.

How? I love John Donne's answer to this in the seventeenth century when he wrote "Meditation Seventeen":

> No man is an island, entire of itself. Every man is a
> piece of the continent, a part of the main. If a clod be
> washed away by the sea, Europe is the less, as well as if
> a promontory were, as well as if a manor of thy friend's
> or of thine own were. Any man's death diminishes
> me, because I am involved in mankind, and therefore
> never send to know for whom the bell tolls; it tolls for
> thee …
>   If by this consideration of another's danger, I take
> mine own into contemplation, and so secure myself,
> by making my recourse to my God, who is our only
> security.[4]

We can use the cold reality of death occurring in the world and our innate knowledge of our own inevitable death to the benefit of our soul's battles. Leland Ryken, in his commentary on the passage above, writes, "According to Donne, the goal of thinking about someone else's death is to be brought closer to God and heaven by that contemplation."[5]

How does this work? Ryken mentions later in the same book the medieval practice of contemplating a "death's head," a real or painted

---

4 Donne, "Meditation Seventeen."

5 Ryken, *Devotional Poetry*, 42.

skull, "as a means of thinking about one's own mortality."[6] Certainly, times have changed since then. The prevalent view in our world is that we must avoid thinking about our mortality, not seek to do so. As I found out on November 1, 2018, facing it is not easy. So why should we?

How can meditating on our own death help us? It forces us to make real in our souls the belief that this life is not all there is. It forces us to bank on our motto that the best is yet to be. In short, it keeps us honest, and it grounds us in reality. It forces us to think of eternity. As Samuel Johnson famously said, "When a man knows he is to be hanged in a fortnight, it concentrates the mind wonderfully."[7]

There is a solid New Testament example of how the nearness of death brings our priorities into focus. We see this in the life and ministry of Paul. One verse he wrote in the letter to the Philippians has bothered me for years. Paul wrote, "For to me to live is Christ, and to die is gain" (1:21). How can that be? First, the word *Christ* is not an adjective. Grammatically, the meaning of the first part of the verse is not immediately apparent. Secondly, isn't it a bit depressing when people view death as gain? Doesn't that paint a bleak picture of our earthly lives?

When I found out I was undeniably afraid to die I realized that I am not really believing that to die is gain. I know it must be true, but deep down in my human heart I just cannot trust that what death brings will be everything it's supposed to be. An unblinking contemplation of my own death, if I venture to undertake it, only leaves me with two options: to sink into despair or to take hold of all that Christ promises me and believe wholeheartedly that "to depart and be with Christ … is far better" (1:23).

---

6 Ryken, 72.

7 Boswell, *Life of Samuel Johnson*, vol. 3, entry from September 19, 1777.

Let's remember that Paul's hope, and ours, is not for a disembodied existence with Christ after death. As Paul wrote later in the letter, "But our citizenship is in heaven, and from it we await a Savior, the Lord Jesus Christ, who will transform our lowly body to be like his glorious body, by the power that enables him even to subject all things to himself" (3:20). He was banking on what N. T. Wright calls "life after life after death"—that is, life in the resurrected body.[8] Our ultimate hope is to be with Christ in our resurrected bodies, in a new earth.

This discussion was particularly pertinent to Paul because of the circumstances in which he wrote the letter. He wrote it around AD 62 while in prison waiting to hear the outcome of his trial on capital charges. This fact gives his writings on death a particular poignancy and value. The entire letter is "written in death's shadow."[9] It was, literally, a life-or-death question, and this dramatically changes how we read the book of Philippians. The reflections that Paul puts to papyrus are prompted by the prospect of his own death. Paul's famous words about Jesus in 2:8 ("obedient to the point of death, even death on a cross") now make me wonder if Paul was holding up that example in front of himself. His words about contentment in all circumstances (4:12) gain a gravitas we would not award to this statement from a person living an easier life.

So one alternative, death, has become "gain" for Paul: he is not afraid of it and the contemplation of it invigorates his hope in Christ. What about the other alternative outcome: if Paul should go on living? He wrote, "To live is Christ, to die is gain" (1:21)—how do these two phrases go together? At first, it seems like these are two alternatives pitted against each other, especially when he wrote, "Yet which I shall choose I cannot tell. I am hard pressed between the two" (1:22–23). In fact, Paul is setting up both possibilities as good options. He's saying it's a win-win either way. He can't lose, alive or dead.

---

8 Wright, *Paul and the Faithfulness*, 113.
9 Kirk, *Departure of an Apostle*, 186.

How does Paul's contemplation of his death inform his perspective on his earthly life before he dies? He says, "To live is Christ." What does "to live is Christ" even mean? We tend to answer that being a Christian and having a personal relationship with Christ makes life on earth not only bearable but good. Jesus comforts us in our afflictions and knowing the truths in his word helps us process all that occurs in the world around us.

This is certainly true, and we can support this interpretation with an abundance of other verses and themes in the Bible, even in Philippians itself. But maybe, in reading the verse this way, we are missing something. Perhaps "to live is Christ" isn't only about our own individual, devotional delights in knowing Christ. Perhaps it encompasses even more. As Lilias Trotter wrote in 1895, "A flower that stops short at its flowering misses its purpose. We were created for more than our own spiritual development; reproduction, not mere development, is the goal of matured being—reproduction in other lives."[10] In other words, we're not meant simply to blossom in the light of Christ but to be fruitful. The prospect of death not only calls us to strengthen our faith in Christ and hope for a future with him beyond death, but it also changes the way we live. It motivates us to live fruitfully.

Was there more to the meaning of "to live is Christ" for Paul—more than just that knowing Jesus gave him personal joy? He explained himself a bit more in the next verse. "If I am to live in the flesh, that means fruitful labor for me" (1:22). Paul's understanding of "to live is Christ" involves his work. He was thinking in terms of his calling to spread the gospel and strengthen the believers. As my husband noted in his dissertation about Paul, "A reading that is more sensitive to the immediate context would be to understand Paul's statement 'to live is Christ' as a distillation of his ministry. His life in the flesh is entirely consumed with proclaiming Christ and teaching about Christ."[11] The

---

10 Trotter, *Parables of the Cross*, 29.

11 Kirk, *Departure of an Apostle*, 196–97.

advantage of staying alive, the remaining tie that bound Paul to earth, was his continuing opportunity to labor for the gospel of Jesus Christ.

The American Board of Missions used to have for its seal an ox, with an altar on one side and a plow on the other, with the motto, "Ready for either." The workers going out under that seal were prepared either to live and labor for Christ or to suffer and die for him.

The first obstacle when I read this verse, of course, is that I am not Paul. My reasons for wanting to continue to live are different than his. In the 1987 film *Princess Bride*, when the farm boy Wesley was brought to Miracle Max because he was "mostly dead," Max, pumping him full of air with a huge old bellows, asked, "What's so important? What you got here that's worth living for?" When he pushes the air out of Wesley, Wesley moans, "True love." Max agreed, "Sonny, true love is the greatest thing in the world. Except for a nice MLT, a mutton, lettuce, and tomato sandwich."

I think some of my reasons for wanting to live are noble, like true love, and some are on the level of a mutton, lettuce, and tomato sandwich—just enjoyment of life on earth in all its salty delights. Remember the cliché about near-death experiences causing your entire life to flash before your eyes? As it turns out, it's a real thing; it's called life review. Apparently for many this phenomenon highlights the events and people who are most important, those connected with our most poignant emotions. I did not experience life review, but in the moments after the stroke struck me, I perceived with utter clarity my biggest reasons for staying alive: my children. I was not thinking about good books, coffee, beaches, or Bach. My thought was, I have to be here for the children. I can identify with Paul; it isn't just being here—it's that I feel my labor for my children is not done. For many of us, our reasons for wanting to live are good reasons.

Paul then wrote of his certainty in predicting that he will live longer because there is more fruitful work for him to do, particularly on behalf of the Philippians themselves: "I know that I will remain and continue with you all, for your progress and joy in the faith, so that in me you may have ample cause to glory in Christ Jesus, because of my coming to you again" (1:25–26). Paul was right about this. Though he did die in Roman hands some years later, the imprisonment during which he wrote Philippians eventually resulted in his being released—and returning to work.

Should not every Christian be able to say, "For me to live is Christ and to die is gain"? Should we all not view our lives in these terms? Or was this unique to Paul, who had an undoubtedly unique role to play in history? Paul seemed fairly confident that the Philippians themselves should interpret their lives' purpose in terms of their gospel labor:

> Only let your *manner of life* be worthy of the gospel
> of Christ, so that whether I come and see you or am
> absent, I may hear of you that you are standing firm in
> one spirit, with one mind, *striving side by side for the*
> *faith of the gospel*, and not frightened in anything by
> your opponents. (1:27–28)

Paul connected for them that living is a joyful service to Christ and that death—far better—is a departure to be with Christ. Living in this matrix results in facing it all—all the options, all the complexity—with Christian courage.

This, then, is the mystery of Philippians. This is the reason why a letter written from a first-century prison by a man awaiting imminent violent death is "one of the most radiantly joyful and mission-focused letters in all of early Christianity."[12]

What "to live is Christ" means is that life, *knowing Christ*, aware of and attached to him, *is* good. He is what makes life good. He must be the reason we cling to life—because life with him, even in a scary world, is life indeed. We invest our lives, our moments and days, our values and joys, our hopes and dreams, our work and effort, in him.

---

12 Kirk, 186.

Sacred Courage

He is what makes life worth living. And when our life ends, whether awash in Legos on our family room floor at thirty-eight or in our sleep at ninety-four, we *gain* because we go to him. The day will come when, in the words of Robert Browning, "death has done all death can."[13] And then—O, then—real life begins.

Could it be that my stroke—this sudden, terrible event that rocked my world and left me with PTSD, fears, and physical challenges that I did not (and do not) want—could be the catalyst for forcing my delinquent soul to grasp hope in Christ, even way down in those deep and broken parts where I wouldn't otherwise have let him in? Could our fear of death and our increasing sense of mortality bring us to the point of finally, wholeheartedly trusting God with that hardest of all things to relinquish—our own lives?

---

13 Browning, *Men and Women*.

Discussion Questions

1. Does your culture or subculture sanitize death? How?

2. What do we gain by contemplating our own death? What can the knowledge that we will die do for us?

3. If you were to fill in the blanks of this statement for yourself, what would the honest answers be? For me, to live is _____, to die is _____.

A Vision of a Dread-Free Life

Walking at liberty, in holy service, in sacred communion, in constant progress in holiness, enjoying the smile of heaven—this I seek after. Here is the loftiest reach of a good man's ambition, to dwell with God, to walk in righteousness before him, to rejoice in his presence, and in the light and glory which it yields.

—Charles Spurgeon, *The Treasury of David*

I married an optimist. It was kind of accidental; I'm not sure how well I understood this aspect of his personality back then or what a significant difference it would show itself to be. For him, the glass isn't just half full. Whatever the glass is half full of is exactly what we need and is exactly the right temperature. There's probably even a little extra to give away. We won't need any more than this, and if we do, there will be more somehow. He's thankful for the glass—it's a nice glass—and he's thankful for its contents.

Not so his wife. He says I'm a pessimist; I say I'm a realist. The glass is half empty. We might as well admit it. We cannot guarantee its contents will be enough, so it behooves us to spend some time developing backup plans to refill it. We should not pick up the glass because glasses drop and break all the time, and we don't have a backup plan for that scenario either. I recognize the futility of asking how we can be sure this is even the best glass since it appears to be the only option, but it's a temptation to ask it anyway.

It isn't that I really believe everything will turn out worst-case scenario. I just believe, based on a lifetime of experience in a broken world, it is always a possibility. Training myself to expect it is just a matter of self-protection. I need to manage my expectations to prevent disappointment if what we're both hoping for doesn't materialize. Because he's an optimist and won't do this for himself, I have the additional burden of needing to manage his expectations too. There's always pie in his sky, and I'm always raining on his parade, to use the words of our glorious (and sometimes incomprehensible) English idioms.

I admire authentic optimists. I think I'm jealous of them. It must be nice to live confident that everything is going to be okay and that circumstances will turn out for the best. They probably don't have that tightness in the chest gripping them in tense times or have the pattern of cracks in the bedroom ceiling memorized. But the truth is, optimists are often fearful too; they just cope with it in different ways.

Have you ever wondered what it would be like to live entirely without fear? To patiently await future developments with quiet confidence in a positive outcome? What would it be like to live unburdened by fear and free from dread? I can only faintly imagine it. There is the feeblest echo of it reaching us through the hundreds of generations of fearful men and women that have trod this sod since Eden. There is the haziest vision of it ahead, in the vague descriptions of a future blessed reality about which we can only imagine.

There are two times in the Bible in which human beings live utterly without fear. The first is in the garden of Eden before the serpent approaches the woman. Adam and Eve are living an idyllic existence in a garden paradise where their communion with God is unbroken, and they don't even know what fear is.

The second time is life in the new heavens and new earth, foreshadowed in Leviticus 26:3–6:

> If you walk in my statutes and observe my
> commandments and do them, then I will give you
> your rains in their season, and the land shall yield
> its increase, and the trees of the field shall yield their
> fruit. Your threshing shall last to the time of the grape
> harvest, and the grape harvest shall last to the time for

sowing. And you shall eat your bread to the full and
dwell in your land securely. I will give peace in the
land, and you shall lie down, and none shall make you
afraid.

An existence in which "none shall make you afraid" is a key part of the
vision for a blessed life. This vision of dwelling securely will only be
fully realized when Jesus returns and God dwells with us, as described
in Revelation 21:1–3:

Then I saw a new heaven and a new earth, for the first
heaven and the first earth had passed away, and the sea
was no more. And I saw the holy city, new Jerusalem,
coming down out of heaven from God, prepared as
a bride adorned for her husband. And I heard a loud
voice from the throne saying, "Behold, the dwelling
place of God is with man. He will dwell with them,
and they will be his people, and God himself will be
with them as their God."

In the garden, there was no fear until communion with God was broken.
When God finally and fully dwells intimately with his people in the
new heavens and new earth, there will be nothing to fear ever again.
These are two swift glimpses, two visionary descriptions bookending
the Bible, of life utterly without fear.

But what about now? As one of my mentors once said, "There's
an awful lot of daily in the meantime!" Is it possible to live here and
now fear free? What would that even look like? I think any vision of
how life could be in the time between the beginning and the end of
earthly human experience must have some allowance for fear. We will
not be totally without a hint of it, without even a possibility of feeling
afraid, until that great day described in Revelation 21. As we have seen
in chapter 1, fears arise and will arise because that is the reality of being
human in this world. The day without fear is coming, but it is not yet.

But can we envision a life in which fear begins to lose its sting, just as death has had its stinger removed by the cross and resurrection of Jesus? Is it possible to live a dread-free life in the middle time—the time we occupy—between the first and second comings of Jesus? A life in which fear, when it arises, is shouldered by our Savior in the same way he carries our guilt and shame? Can we walk forward in faith on a path that gets not darker and darker but genuinely "brighter and brighter until full day" (Prov 4:18)?

We need a vision that allows for the perpetual arising of fear but not for living under its burden. This side of heaven, a dread-free life involves a faith characterized by endurance and patience—"all endurance and patience with joy," as Paul put it in Colossians 1:11. It requires a robust response to fear that does not cripple us with doubt and hopelessness yet gives us repeated opportunities to revel anew in all that we have in Christ Jesus.

The famous godly woman described in Proverbs 31 illustrates this vision. She is many things: diligent, industrious, creative, generous, helpful, and trustworthy. But most notably to me, she is not afraid of the future. It says of her in verse 25, "Strength and dignity are her clothing, and she laughs at the time to come." Fear of the future does not steal her joy.

What we call fear of the future is really fear of what the future *may* bring. What if this happens, and what if that happens? In other words, we're asking the "what if" questions. Have you noticed how many of our fears begin with a real or implied "What if …?" These kinds of questions will arise, and worrying over each one takes emotional energy, increases our anxiety, and steals our hope.

I am an expert at what-ifs, and I descend from a long line of skilled what-iffers. We can generate an impressive list of potential catastrophes for nearly every human decision. When you get really good you can make a string of these: "What if I don't do well on this project?" becomes "What if I lose my job?" becomes "What if I can never get another one?" becomes "What if I have to move into my parents' basement and live there forever?"

Twice so far, during particularly difficult times in my life journey, my skill at asking terrifying what-if questions reached truly prodigious heights. Both times I was walking through some scary territory, and both times God eventually brought something to my attention that helped me with my fear of the future. I share these stories of my experience of God's grace to illustrate what a dread-free life could look like in practice.

The first time of difficulty was when we were preparing to move to Southeast Asia. I had never seen the country to which we were moving. I could not join my husband on a preparatory trip because I was expecting our fourth child. At the time of our move, our older children were six, four, and two years of age and the baby less than a year old—too young for basic vaccinations. We were moving to the world's largest Muslim country and beginning a new life for which I felt ill-equipped and inadequate. I could have written five volumes of my what-if questions. I could have made a fortune selling the film rights to the scary movies in my head.

At this time, in God's mercy, the women's ministry at our church asked me to share some testimony from my life at an event. As I prepared, I realized how much of my story was about fear and how much of my fears were just projected what-ifs. I started searching my Bible to see what it could tell me about what-if questions. It was a somewhat frustrating search. Often the verses containing the word *if* ended up not being about fear at all. In fact, they often were promises. I kept reading them, trying to find evidence to make my point, and found instead God was making his.

There was a curious parallel between many of my what-if fears and the "ifs" in the Bible. My gut-wrenching question, "What if moving our whole family so far away is a big mistake that somehow ruins our lives?"

was answered with, "*If* I take the wings of the morning and dwell in the uttermost parts of the sea, even there your hand shall lead me and your right hand shall hold me" (Ps 139:9–10). It seemed every one of my biggest what-ifs had an "if" from the Bible that silenced it. Try this sometime when you need it. I've started you off with a list I made.

Table 1: What-If Fears and the Bible's Responses

What-If Fears	The Bible's "If ..." Responses
What if God can't forgive me?	If we confess our sins, he is faithful and just to forgive us our sins and to cleanse us from all unrighteousness. (1 John 1:9)
What if I'm not really saved?	If you confess with your mouth that Jesus is Lord and believe in your heart that God raised him from the dead, you will be saved. (Rom 10:9)
What if I'm stuck in sin?	If anyone does sin, we have an advocate with the Father, Jesus Christ the righteous. (1 John 2:1) If the Son sets you free, you will be free indeed. (John 8:36)
What if I'm always alone? What if I end up alone?	If what you heard from the beginning abides in you, then you too will abide in the Son and in the Father. (1 John 2:24)
What if my needs aren't met?	If God so clothes the grass of the field, which today is alive and tomorrow is thrown into the oven, will he not much more clothe you, O you of little faith? (Matt 6:30)

What if I miss out on good things?	If you then, who are evil, know how to give good gifts to your children, how much more will your Father who is in heaven give good things to those who ask him! (Matt 7:11)
What if things get really hard? What if I suffer?	If [we are] children, then heirs—heirs of God and fellow heirs with Christ, provided we suffer with him in order that we may also be glorified with him. (Rom 8:17)
What if I am attacked? What if my family is attacked?	If God is for us, who can be against us? (Rom 8:31) If it had not been the LORD who was on our side when people rose up against us, then they would have swallowed us up alive.... Blessed be the LORD, who has not given us a prey to their teeth! (Ps 124:2–3, 6)
What if I die?	If we live, we live to the Lord, and if we die, we die to the Lord. So then, whether we live or whether we die, we are the Lord's. (Rom 14:8)
What if I can't handle it (whatever it is)? What if I don't measure up?	[Yet if so] God is able to make all grace abound to you, so that having all sufficiency in all things at all times, you may abound in every good work. (2 Cor 9:8)

What if these promises are for me? Dear reader, every word of them is true for you and for me in Jesus Christ. "For all the promises of God find their Yes in him" (2 Cor 1:20). As I rediscovered these promises I was flooded with a profound reassurance in the faithfulness of God. In their light, the shadow of dread I had been laboring under was dissipated. I shared every one of them with the women at the church event. It was because I was clinging tightly to these promises in my heart that I could move to the other side of the world a few months later.

The second time I caught a glimpse of the vision of what life unburdened by dread could look like was after the stroke I experienced in Indonesia in November 2018. The stroke was the most traumatic event I had ever experienced, and I learned in the aftermath that it had left a momentous and volcanic impact on my heart, mind, and body. Trauma is when *what-if* happens. It moves us into an entirely new realm of fear and anxiety. It taught me, as I began to exhibit symptoms of PTSD, that we have little control over our body's reactions to trauma. The what-if questions began again with new intensity, and I felt like I was being devoured by anxiety.

In those long months of recovery, I dug into books for help. Surely in my reading there would be some answers to my situation. Surely some of those authors I admire and from whose writings I have gained insight would have written about this. Many of them faced far greater traumas than the one that had so swiftly knocked me off my feet.

For example, what about Elisabeth Elliot? In the early 1950s, Elisabeth Elliot and her husband Jim moved to the jungles of Ecuador to bring the gospel of Jesus Christ. Early in their service, Jim and four teammates were killed by the natives they were attempting to reach. What I really want to know about Elisabeth is this: how did she live with the aftermath of that trauma? Did she wake up shaking in the night with nightmares, locked in a silent terror, not sure what to do or whom to call for help, and crying out to God on the inside? Did she wrestle with the questions of whether to take a pill, say a prayer, do both, or do neither— not confident either one would be helpful? I needed to ask her that—but she went to be with Jesus a month before we moved to Indonesia, so I will have to wait. What would she say to me?

If living an authentic life on earth unburdened by the dread of the future is possible, then I must believe it is also possible for people who have experienced trauma. At least the dream—the vision of it—is out there in front of us, motivating us in the fight for faith. It is why we don't just give up and give in to fear.

About three months after the stroke, we were visiting an older couple who works for our organization. When the wife asked me how I was doing, I told her about my increased anxiety.

"My mind and body are constantly asking me, over and over, 'What if I have another stroke right now? What about now? Now?'" I said. "I'm so desperately tired of it!"

"You can't stop that question from coming," she said. "But be sure to finish the conversation. Answer it every time. What if you had another stroke right now? Was God with you the first time? Will he be with you again? If that happens to you, can God still be working all things out for your good? What's the worst that could happen: What if you die? What if you do? What can you expect next?"

This friend gave me a flashing glimpse of what true, unshakable hope in things certain that we cannot see can do for the soul that possesses it (Heb 11:1). It is *liberty*. Every what-if, however terrible, that can occur in the life of one of God's own cannot uproot it from the bedrock of God's certain and faithful promises. The soul that grasps this is free indeed. Fear, where then is your sting? This has become part of my profile of someone who "laughs at the time to come" (Prov 31:25): someone who answers every what-if question with "even so."

So I began to discipline my traumatized mind to answer every "what-if" with "even so." What if I have another stroke? I can't go through that again. Even so, God will be with me. What if I'm disabled, and I'll never be the same again? Even so, God has good plans for my life. What if I die? Even so.

Envision a life in which, every time what-if sounds in the soul, it is fully answered with an unshaken "even so." That is the dread-free life. I do not live it yet; I aspire to it. The woman of Proverbs 31 lived the dread-free life. Can we find the vision for this kind of life anywhere else in the Bible?

Sacred Courage

There were many times when the future that appeared to be in store for God's people was not one to laugh at. The book of Habakkuk is a brilliant example. It was written around 600 BC, during an imminent threat in the form of the nation of the Chaldeans, amassing in the northeast. The book begins with a different kind of complaint, however. Habakkuk is lamenting the lack of righteousness and justice in Israel under the depraved king Joachin. "So the law is paralyzed, and justice never goes forth. For the wicked surround the righteous; so justice goes forth perverted" (1:4).

God's answer to Habakkuk isn't the answer for which he is probably hoping. The future is not going to be what he anticipated. God is raising up the ruthless Chaldean army to invade Israel. God reveals to Habakkuk what they are like: "For behold, I am raising up the Chaldeans, that bitter and hasty nation, who march through the breadth of the earth, to seize dwellings not their own. They are dreaded and fearsome" (1:6–7). Things were going to get a lot worse before they got better.

Habakkuk is horrified to learn that this is God's plan. He realizes that God is raising up this enemy as a judgment over Israel. Now, in his second complaint, he asks how this is consistent with God's character:

> O LORD, you have ordained them as a judgment, and
> you, O Rock, have established them for reproof. You
> who are of purer eyes than to see evil and cannot look
> at wrong, why do you idly look at traitors and remain
> silent when the wicked swallows up the man more
> righteous than he? (1:12–13)

God answers him by telling him to write down the vision that fills most of the rest of the book. It is a litany of judgment against the unrighteous, ending with these words, "But the LORD is in his holy temple; let all the earth keep silence before him" (2:20).

As Habakkuk begins his prayer in chapter 3, he is in a fearful state: "O LORD, I have heard the report of you, and your work, O LORD, do I fear" (v. 2). As he considers all that God has done and can do, he describes the physiological effects of this fear gripping him: "I hear, and my body trembles; my lips quiver at the sound; rottenness enters into my bones; my legs tremble beneath me" (3:16). Israel is no safe place for Habakkuk, and the day of deliverance has not come. He is living with great fear of current and future events. But verse 16 continues, "Yet I will quietly wait for the day of trouble to come upon people who invade us." His posture is one of *quietly waiting* for God to show himself just. Talk about realistic optimism!

Here is one of the greatest depictions of the dread-free life between Eden and the new earth. The final verses are filled with projections—the what-ifs of Habakkuk's world and his resounding, musical "even so":

> Though the fig tree should not blossom,
>   nor fruit be on the vines,
>
> the produce of the olive fail
>   and the fields yield no food,
>
> the flock be cut off from the fold
>   and there be no herd in the stalls,
>
> yet I will rejoice in the LORD;
>   I will take joy in the God of my salvation.
>
> GOD, the Lord, is my strength;
>   he makes my feet like the deer's;
>   he makes me tread on my high places.
>
> To the choirmaster: with stringed instruments.
>   (3:17–19)

I loved these verses when they were the text for the homily at our wedding in 2004, but I love them so much more today. This isn't a blind, Pollyanna-style optimism that thinks everything is always hunky-dory.

Habakkuk knows it isn't, and he knows it won't be. But he has found a faith that secures him on the scary heights. He waits in quietness for the salvation of the Lord. I mentioned earlier that Paul's prayer for the Colossians involved them having endurance and patience—it actually says, "all endurance and patience with joy" (1:11). Habakkuk isn't tortured by the "what ifs" in his future. Amazingly, miraculously, he's found joy.

This vision of a life, amid a world warped and broken yet radiating Christian courage and unshaken confidence in an inevitable triumphant outcome, moves me to the depths. This is optimism of the best and truest sort, not blind to adversity but viewing it from a perspective that sees above and beyond it. In short, it is joy that is durable. It can withstand the wear and tear—and the direct and violent onslaught—that comes with facing all the heartaches and losses of life on earth, whether they occur or merely hang overhead as possibilities. I want a joy that won't wear out from daily use—joy woven from the sturdy cords of confidence in the promises that are yes in Jesus. The woman who has that joy can smile at the future.

Sometimes doesn't your heart just cry, "Oh, to be free! To be *free* of it! I don't want to live like this anymore"? It's a miserable, shrinking existence to live tortured by anxiety. Accumulated fear is a massive burden, and it feels like we are forever bound by it. Don't you wish we could just cut it loose? Can you imagine what it would feel like to face the future and know you're invincible, that nothing can touch you?

Don't tell me it can't be done. Do not tell me it's unrealistic. I'll tell you something realistic: Jesus died for this. He rose again so we could say "O Death, where is thy sting?" Surely he meant us to say that to fear, too? If the freedom gained on the cross means anything, it means everything, and it must mean we're aiming far too low in our struggles with fear.

Our goal ought not to be managing anxiety or treating it or coping with it or controlling it or medicating it. Let's overcome it!

Merely managing fear is not how you become the Proverbs 31 woman. The Proverbs 31 woman "*laughs* at the time to come" (v. 25). She's facing the future and saying, "Bring it on!" You don't say that unless you're ready for whatever it can bring you.

We've already considered the prevalence of fear in our world and that the way to confront it is not by analyzing it or reasoning ourselves out of it. We have seen how fear itself is not a sin, but it continually presents us with an opportunity to trust God, especially the fear of death. In this chapter, we have considered what a faithful life in a fearful realm could look like for the believer. In the chapters ahead we will consider how faith might move us from a state of fearfulness to striding forward in courage, confident in our God.

What if … ?

Even so!

Discussion Questions

1. Can you imagine your life free from dread? How would it be different?

2. Do you think it is possible? Why or why not?

3. What is your biggest "what-if" right now? Can you craft an "even so" sentence or find an "if" promise to cling to when you begin to ask it?

6

The Fear of the Lord

> "The Fear?" the king said. He smiled a thin smile and wet
> the end of one finger in the wine.
> "It is the name my people use for God," the boy said.
> "I fear nothing," the king said. "If I find something that is to
> be feared, I destroy it."
> "The king does not fear the gods?" the boy said.
> "I do not fear them, I feed them," the king said.
> —Frederick Buechner, *Son of Laughter*

> O most mighty God, and merciful God, the God of all true
> sorrow, and true joy too, of all fear, and of all hope too, as
> thou hast given me a repentance, not to be repented of, so
> give me, O Lord, a fear, of which I may not be afraid.
> —John Donne, *Meditations, Prayer VI*

In chapter 5 we briefly looked at the Proverbs 31 woman, who nobly embodies the many virtues described at the end of Proverbs. There is much to appreciate in this person, but the facet of her character that I admire most is described in verse 25: "Strength and dignity are her clothing, and she laughs at the time to come." Can you see the strength of this woman? What people wear is visible—we notice the colors, shapes, and styles of the garments of the women around us without even trying. Far from the prevalent caricature of the Christian woman, who is a mealymouthed doormat kept firmly in a servile role by old-fashioned dogma and dominant males, this woman is strong. Her strength and honor are evident, so much a part of her that she is wearing them like a good pair of jeans and a new shirt. In her strong posture, there is no hint of shrinking, cowering, or keeping her eyes lowered.

She's staring straight ahead, and she's laughing. She is walking forward, free of fear's heaviness. Even though life on earth must bring her pain and suffering, she's a biblical example of a woman living the vision of a dread-free life described in the previous chapter.

How did she get there? (How do *we* get there?) I believe the key to her strength and laughter is revealed at the end of Proverbs 31. What is the most important thing about this woman? The final descriptive sentence about the woman functions as a summary statement. It comes after the long list of her virtues and activities, after the voices of her children and husband praising her. It is as if the author wants to ensure we don't miss the most significant element of who she is: "Charm is deceptive and beauty is vain, but a woman who fears the LORD is to be praised" (v. 30). Proverbs 31:30 is what makes the life of Proverbs 31:25 possible. Furthermore, because verse 30 comes at the end of the book, it can be understood as a summary of the entire book as well. It highlights for us one of its central themes: the fear of the Lord.[1]

The Proverbs 31 description is not the first place where a life without dread is mentioned in the book. Interestingly, the book opens with the same idea. First, we are clearly told that the fear of the Lord is the beginning of wisdom in 1:7. The link between fearing the Lord and wisdom is reiterated in chapter 2 when the author writes that those who seek wisdom and understanding "will understand the fear of the LORD and find the knowledge of God" (v. 5). In chapter 1, wisdom is personified as a woman calling out in the streets to whoever will listen to her (vv. 20–21). She predicts disaster will come upon those who do not heed her "because they hated knowledge and did not choose the fear of the LORD" (v. 29). But what does she promise to those who listen? What is their reward of surpassing worth? She says, "Whoever listens to me will dwell secure and will be at ease, *without dread of disaster*" (1:33). A dread-free life, according to Proverbs, is one marked by the fear of the Lord, which is true wisdom and understanding.

---

1 See Proverbs 1:7, 29; 2:5; 8:13; 9:10; 10:27; 14:26, 27; 15:16, 33; 16:6; 19:23; 22:4; 23:17; 29:25.

Here we find one of the biggest paradoxes in our paradox-filled faith: to live in victory over fear we must have fear—that is, fear of the Lord. What does this phrase mean? Are we supposed to be scared of God? Is it just an acknowledgment of God's bigness, his power, his ability to do "all that he pleases" (Ps 115:3)? Is it reverence?

Reverence fits well with how Muslims understand this concept. The fear of Allah is at the core of Islam. He is so very high. To show your fear of Allah, you must keep your promises to him. The Qur'an says, "Whoever fulfills his pledge and fears Allah much; verily, then Allah loves those who are Al-Muttaqun [promise-keepers]."[2] A true believer will "fulfill his pledge" and thus demonstrate his proper fear of Allah. The emphasis is on the believer keeping his promises to Allah. For Muslims, fearing God involves the placation and appeasement of a supreme power. But what does it mean for us?

Certainly, fearing God does involve a recognition of his power. In the first chapter, we saw from the Gospel of Mark that a powerful figure can only be defeated by a more powerful figure, and the most powerful figure is the one to fear. This is why the people and the disciples transferred their fear of the man possessed by a legion of demons to Jesus when Jesus cast out the demons. This is why they were suddenly terrified of Jesus after he calmed the storm. They recognized him as the most powerful figure, the one of whom to be afraid.

Jesus reinforces this directly in his teachings as recorded by Matthew. He says, "And do not fear those who kill the body but cannot kill the soul. Rather fear him who can destroy both soul and body in hell" (10:28). I don't think Jesus mentions hell in this verse because he wants to hold it over our heads and make us scared. Notice how he continues in the next verse: "Are not two sparrows sold for a penny? And not one of them will fall to the ground apart from your Father. But even the hairs of your head are all numbered. Fear not, therefore; you are of more value than many sparrows" (10:29–31). In verse 28, I think Jesus is urging us to focus our attention on the most powerful figure—not on our human

---

2 *Surah Al-Imran* 3:76.

enemies but on the one who would be the most formidable enemy of all if he *was* our enemy—God. So Jesus is also telling us not to fear earthly threats or enemies but to fear only God, whose power supersedes theirs.

Likewise, in the book of Isaiah, when the Assyrian invasion is threatening Israel, the prophet declares:

> For the LORD spoke thus to me with his strong hand
> upon me, and warned me not to walk in the way of
> this people, saying: "Do not call conspiracy all that
> this people calls conspiracy, and do not fear what they
> fear, nor be in dread. But the LORD of hosts, him you
> shall honor as holy. Let him be your fear, and let him
> be your dread." (8:11–13)

There are formidable human enemies in the offing, but God presents himself as the one to be feared, the most powerful figure. It is not that other powers are not real or not frightening; it is that compared to God's total power, unrivaled authority, and utter sovereignty, these other powers aren't important. It is that "He that seeth God by a spirit of faith in his greatness and power, he sees all other things below as nothing."[3]

Fearing God means, for starters, that we have focused our fear on him because ultimately he will determine all outcomes. This view puts all other threats to our security in proper perspective. Many people have written that the one that fears God fears nothing and no one else, but John Donne took it a step further when he wrote, "As he that fears God, fears nothing else, so he that sees God sees everything else."[4] The knowledge of God and fear of him lowers everything else to its proper place. Seeing God rightly will inform our perspective on all other threats and dangers.

Yet I think fearing God involves more than simply discerning the true power structure in the universe. We must also realize that wisdom

---

3 Richard Sibbs, as quoted by Spurgeon, *Treasury of David*, 1:7.

4 Donne, *Works of John Donne*, 4:238.

and understanding—the "knowledge of God" and an appreciation of the full range of his true character (Prov 2:5)—are crucial to fearing the Lord. In other words, we must let the Bible, as it teaches us about God's true character, fill out for us this concept of fearing the Lord. If the fear of the Lord is the key to living a dread-free life, we must not draw an unbiblically narrow picture of what this fear of him is. As we grow in our understanding of the relationship God wants to have with us, we will know what it is to fear him.

In my own journey, God brought me to the point of at least intellectually understanding we must fear God—and shouldn't fear anything else—by my early thirties. But I was operating from a paradigm that thought fearing God almost exclusively meant having reverence for him, particularly his sovereignty and power. Of course, at that time I knew Proverbs 1:7, "The fear of the LORD is the beginning of wisdom." I did feel the acute need for wisdom for two reasons: First, we had just added our third child within four years. (I will not explain that one to you.) Second, we were facing the biggest unknown of my life. Yet I hadn't yet realized how fearing God could lead to wisdom, instead of reverence or humility. There was a deficiency in my understanding of what it means to fear the Lord.

I wrote in chapter 1 about sensing that God was leading me to serve overseas. When I married my husband, we had that sense in common. What we did not have in common were our feelings about it. I believe that Alex was honestly ready to follow God anywhere—he thought the life of Jim Elliot, for example, was a particularly inspiring one. He didn't seem to have many questions or hesitancies about what a life of overseas service could mean, and I never heard him voice any fears about it.

Not so his wife. I did feel that God was clearly leading us both overseas, but I felt neither delighted nor excited about this. My ambitions did not include being speared in the jungle for the glory of God, and I was pretty sure I had not been given the spiritual gift of self-sacrifice. Fear was a powerful, though unacknowledged, stronghold in my life. It gave me all kinds of reasons to stay home. I was stuck on the horns of the dilemma between obedience to God's call and my own strong reluctance to go anywhere unfamiliar.

As a sort of self-protection, I created all kinds of boundaries around what I would and would not do: "I will not go until I'm ready. I will not be gone from home for too many years at a time and not see our families. I will not go anywhere that is not safe. I will never go to a Muslim country." I laid these down emphatically, even angrily, as we talked about our future. I fiercely tried to control the scenario in which I would, should my conditions be met, be obedient. Alex (rashly, as I thought) committed to me that we would never go anywhere I did not want to go. I told him he would just have to trust God to change my heart if we didn't agree on a place because I was *not* going if I didn't want to. (As it turns out, that was the only thing I got right. Eventually, God did change my heart.)

We had known when we married that we needed to pay down college debt before going, and Alex wanted to pursue higher education. We also hoped to have children. There were some big gaps in our plan, particularly regarding how we were going to support ourselves if I was caring for our children and Alex was studying full time. (I could tell you many tales of God's provision in how this unfolded.) We called our plans for this stage of life our "ten-year plan."

In God's providence, the ten-year plan basically happened. We were married in 2004. After both working and paying down debt, Alex pursued a second master's degree and a PhD. We had three kids. However, by late 2012, the ten years were nearly up, and we had no idea what came next. God had not yet given us a clear vision of the next year, let alone another ten years into the future. Alex's doctoral program in England would finish in the next few months. We had no house, no car, no assets of any kind, and no savings account. We had no home in

America to which we could return, no jobs, and no medical insurance. We still wanted to move overseas, but we didn't know where yet, and we hadn't found or joined a sending agency.

I was a mess. I felt (and said) that we were the stupidest, most irresponsible people. Our friends were buying houses, and we had never bought a car. We had said for years that we wanted to go overseas, but we had no idea where or how to get there. My fears told me daily that we'd have to call my dad and ask if we could raise three children in his basement. Fear announced that after all this education we were fit for nothing, that we had chased a nebulous, unprovable sense of inward calling and sacrificed all our prospects for it and were left with nothing. Over the nearly ten years of our marriage, God had begun to pry my fearful fingers off of some of my rules about where I would and would not go, but I was far from peaceful about it.

Alex was full of faith. He was sure that God was going to lead us to the right place, that he would provide what was needed to get there. He worked hard on his dissertation and his part-time job.

Often, we would end up arguing, or I would end up angry. I think it greatly puzzled dear Alex why we couldn't just sit down and have a calm, rational conversation about our future. If I didn't then, I now know why it was. These were "high-stakes" conversations. The things we were talking about were of serious importance and, for me, inextricably connected to fears and anxiety about our future. I just couldn't trust that God would lead us. I felt like we were leading ourselves—right off the map.

We had a clear plan for the first ten years. But now we didn't know what the future would bring. I was so scared of the unknown. I wanted so badly to know where we were going to go and how we were going to get there. I wanted a glimpse of the future.

So what does this have to do with the fear of the Lord? Simply this: I had grasped somehow that the fear of the Lord was the key to a dread-free life. And a dread-free life then, as now, sounded like exactly what I wanted and needed. But I did not understand what the fear of the Lord meant in biblical terms. I equated it merely with *reverence* for God because he's God, but did not also equate it with *trust* in God because he's God. Fear and trust, as John Calvin wrote, "do not seem at first view to harmonize."[5] I knew we needed to fear the Lord in those uncertain days with a hazy future, having no idea what was going to unfold for us. But I did not realize what exactly that meant and how fearing God could help me with my fear of the future.

God used a single verse to unlock for me what fearing God fully means: "The friendship of the LORD is for those who fear him, and he makes known to them his covenant" (Ps 25:14). Astoundingly, we are told here that when we fear the Lord, he offers us friendship. How can we be his friends and afraid of him at the same time? Clearly, fear of the Lord is not the kind of fear that we sometimes have in relationships. We usually think of fear as limiting or damaging the potential of friendship—as in, if I am afraid I can't trust you, then it's hard to be friends. We hesitate to be vulnerable in friendship sometimes because we are afraid of giving the other person more ammunition against us if it turns out they can't be trusted. Have you ever been "burnt" by someone to whom you offered friendship? Probably after that, the fear of being hurt again made the friendship nearly impossible.

But in Psalm 25:14 the friendship of the Lord is specifically for those that fear him. The word translated as "friendship" conveys the idea of secret counsel or close company. It is the idea of receiving confidences— as in Proverbs 3:32, "For the devious person is an abomination to the LORD, but the upright are in his confidence." The word translated as "confidence" in Proverbs 3:32 is the same Hebrew word that is translated as "friendship" in Psalm 25:14. The *ESV Study Bible* says we are "welcome into his intimate company."[6]

---

5 John Calvin, as quoted by Spurgeon, *Treasury of David*, 2:243.
6 *ESV Study Bible*, 968.

In Indonesia everyone has a guest room. It is the first room you enter when you come into the house, always furnished with wooden chairs and a small table. There usually will be a curtain obstructing your view of the rest of the house. If there are public things you are proud of, such as religious icons or Arabic verses or pictures of your children graduating with degrees, they are on display in this room. Everyone that comes inside will be seated here and served sweet jasmine tea. It is only the family and the closest of friends that you invite into the home beyond the curtain. The people that can pass that barrier are those who can know all about you.

I think this Hebrew word for friendship in Psalm 25 is for the kind of people who can freely pass beyond the curtain. Remember, it's describing the kind of friendship available to those who fear the Lord—a friendship where we are brought all the way in to see what he's really up to.

Do we grasp what it means to have a friendship like this with God? It means we are in his inner circle. He has made known to us his secret counsel. The second part of the verse says, "He makes known to them his covenant." The result and proof of God's friendship, then, is him making his covenant intentions known to his people. God's covenant promises are for those who fear him. How different from Islam, in which those who fear Allah are those who keep their promises to him! Those who fear our God are those to whom God makes—and keeps—promises.

There are two Old Testament men who were called friends of God. Both were recipients of God's covenant promises. One was Abraham, who was called God's friend several times. James writes of him, "The Scripture was fulfilled that says, 'Abraham believed God, and it was counted to him as righteousness'—and he was called a friend of God" (2:23). James is referring to 2 Chronicles 20:7 or Isaiah 41:8, both of which note this special relationship. Abraham's friendship with God is evidenced by the fact that Abraham *believed* God—some communication was imparted by God to Abraham and whom Abraham trusted. In the Isaiah passage, God is saying that his people are "the offspring of Abraham, my friend."

Then he continues, "Fear not, for I am with you; be not dismayed, for I am your God; I will strengthen you, I will help you, I will uphold you with my righteous right hand" (41:10). Being God's people, descendants of God's friend, gives them reason not to fear.

The second person described as God's friend is Moses in Exodus 33:11: "Thus the LORD used to speak to Moses face to face, as a man speaks to his friend." Again, the evidence of friendship is the fact that something is being communicated to or confided in Moses by God. Moses is in God's confidence to some extent; God imparts his covenant intentions to Moses. In Deuteronomy 4:7–8, when Moses speaks to the people, he says, "For what great nation is there that has a god so near to it as the LORD our God is to us, whenever we call upon him? And what great nation is there, that has statutes and rules so righteous as all this law that I set before you today?" God's near relationship to his people is demonstrated by the gifting of his covenant to them, as Psalm 25:14 echoes: "The friendship of the LORD is for those who fear him, and he makes known to them his covenant."

If friendship with God was possible for Abraham, Moses, and the psalmist, how much more is it true for us—who have the full revelation of God's image in his Son Jesus Christ? Talk about being welcome beyond the curtain! Do you remember what Jesus said about being friends with us?

> Greater love has no one than this, that someone lay
> down his life for his friends. You are my friends if
> you do what I command you. No longer do I call
> you servants, for the servant does not know what his
> master is doing; but I have called you friends, for all
> that I have heard from my Father I have made known
> to you. (John 15:13–15)

Jesus also defines friendship as close confidence. He says we are his friends because we know what he is doing. God's plans have been made known to us by Jesus, bringing us into a new role as his close companions. Jesus himself has made known to us what the Father is doing. Through his actions and words on earth, he added substantially to the earlier known revelation about God. He himself was "the image of the invisible God" (Col 1:15), and God brought us much more fully into his divine confidence with Jesus's advent. As the author of Hebrews wrote,

> Long ago, at many times and in many ways, God
> spoke to our fathers by the prophets, but in these
> last days he has spoken to us by his Son, whom he
> appointed the heir of all things, through whom he
> also created the world. He is the radiance of the glory
> of God and the exact imprint of his nature, and he
> upholds the universe by the word of his power. (1:1–3)

God made Abraham and Moses his friends by making his covenant known to them. But we have what John Calvin called a "far higher distinction" than even this, "since God hath entirely conveyed himself to us in his son."[7] According to Jesus himself, through him we enter a relationship that supersedes the master-servant dynamics we might expect. (Indeed, many religions are built around this master-servant framework, such as Islam.) Jesus is telling his followers that they

> have a new level of intimacy as friends because they have
> been made privy ... to what Jesus himself knows about
> their future, and what is more, because of Jesus' relation
> with the Father, this is to be made privy to the Father's
> own purposes of love for Jesus and the disciples.[8]

---

7 Calvin, *Gospel according to John*, 2:117–18.

8 Lincoln, *Gospel according to St. John*, 406–7.

In Jesus, we have been brought into the kind of close relationship with God previously only attained by Abraham and Moses.

What is it about God that Jesus makes clear to us, his friends? In Jesus we see proof positive of his good intentions toward us. He remains a God unutterably high and holy with an unimpaired and unimpeachable character. Yet in fantastic condescension, he provides a glorious rescue. We see his unfathomable wisdom, his foreknowledge of all events, and his storm-quenching power. And, as seen in this passage from John 15, we see that he has for us the greatest love possible. At the core of God's friendship with us is specifically the revelation of what he is up to in the death of his Son on our behalf. That tells us everything we need to know.

So the way that the fear of the Lord helps us to fear nothing is that we who fear him not only *tremble* before his power but also *trust* his goodness. In so doing we have his friendship—meaning we have been taken into the confidence of the God of the universe. God has informed us, in advance, of his plans because we are his friends. We, his intimate companions, his covenant people, know our final destiny. We have been privy to God's supreme act of covenant love toward us, and we know that he will allow nothing to undermine, diminish, alter, or cancel its triumphant outcome. We know where this whole universe is headed.

In the previous chapter, I said that many of our fears can take the form of what-if questions. They are projections into the future, things that may or could happen. We are concerned about these things because we do not know, and we cannot control, what will occur in our lives or in the lives of our loved ones. But who holds the future? Whose plan is it? We aren't stumbling along like those who do not know where we are headed, as I mistakenly believed in those uncertain days in England at the end of 2012. I wish I could go back and whisper into my own ear: God has made known to us his secret counsel, and thus, ultimately, we do know the plan. We may not know every particular of it, but we don't need to. We not only know the most powerful figure, but we are also close and intimate companions with him, and he has told us everything we need to know. As Corrie ten Boom said, "Never be afraid to trust an unknown future to a known God."[9] We are friends with the one who knows all the unknowns, who has planned it all, who will carry it all out.

Dear ones, if the Proverbs 31 woman, informed by what she knew of the Lord and his intentions, was laughing at the future, how much deeper ought our chuckles be? We have been made friends of God, and he has confided in us plans for our ultimate good that cannot be canceled or changed. At the inner core of his plan and his very heart is the sacrificial giving of his Son for us. As we fear him, he makes us not only servants but friends and opens his covenant—and his covenant love—to us. It is this experience of his love that dispels our dread.

---

9 Ten Boom, *Clippings from My Notebook*, 27.

Discussion Questions

1. Are you scared of God?

2. How have you understood what it means to fear the Lord?

3. How can you grow in your own friendship with God?

7

God Is a Refuge for Us

> What more do we need for our souls than to have this God
> for our God?
>
> —Lilias Trotter, *Parables of the Cross*

> As the marsh hen secretly builds
> on the watery sod,
> Behold I will build me a nest
> on the greatness of God.
>
> —Sidney Lanier, "The Marshes of Glynn"

It happened when I was about nine years old. We weren't really allowed to be out in the neighborhood alone, and I cannot remember why I was that day. Had I really wandered several streets from our cul-de-sac or was I walking home from playing with a friend? As I walked, I became aware of a car following me. (I've already written that I was a fearful child. I think this fear contributed to a heightened level of awareness of what was happening around me.) All I can remember is that it was a dark-colored sedan, driving slowly, about thirty yards behind me.

At first, I thought maybe the driver was lost, but when I made my next turn, the car did too. My heart started beating faster—I suddenly, inexplicably became convinced that this car somehow meant me harm. There was no one around, and I was still quite a distance from home. I began walking much faster. The car kept the same distance behind. There were still several blocks and several corners to turn before I could sprint for home.

Suddenly I saw that the garage door of a yellow house ahead was standing open. I think my mother knew this family a little and had greeted them before, but I didn't know them at all. Yet somehow when I reached their driveway, my feet turned and I marched confidently up it and straight into the garage as if I lived there. Once inside, I darted behind their car and stooped down in the darkness, waiting to see if my trick worked. Ordinarily, I would have been scared just to enter a stranger's garage, but I was far more afraid of the unnamed threat of that car.

I saw the car slow down as it passed the driveway and hesitate a moment at the end of it. I imagined the driver studying the garage to see where I had gone. Then suddenly the engine roared as it sped away. When it was gone, I found I was shaking. I waited another minute in the darkness before dashing out of that garage and running home for all I was worth.

I am not sure how, at nine years old, I knew what to do. But I made that strange yellow house my own, and it became a refuge for me.

In the previous chapter we sought to understand what the "fear of the LORD" means in biblical terms. Clearly, it cannot mean danger-driven fear because of verses like Proverbs 14:26: "In the fear of the LORD one has strong confidence, and his children will have a refuge." Here we find another great enigma of the Christian faith: the one we fear becomes our refuge. Notice Isaiah 8:13, which says, "But the LORD of hosts, him you shall honor as holy. Let him be your fear, and let him be your dread." This is immediately followed by "And he will become a sanctuary" (8:14). John Calvin said God is "the saints' last asylum."[1] Or, in the words of Martin Luther, "a mighty fortress is our God."[2]

How many times is God called our refuge in the Bible? How many times is he called a fortress, a stronghold, a shield, or a rock? When frightening circumstances arise in the lives of the psalmists, these are the terms they use for God again and again.[3] If you examine the motif of God providing refuge or shelter throughout the Bible, it's everywhere.

---

1 John Calvin, as quoted by Spurgeon, *Treasury of David*, 1:443.

2 Further lines of Luther's renowned hymn are "A sure stronghold our God is he / A timely shield and weapon; / Our help he'll be and set us free / From every ill can happen."

3 According to my own count in the ESV, God is called a "refuge" 44 times, a "fortress" 14 times, a "stronghold" 7 times, a "shield" 17 times, and a "rock" 21 times in the book of Psalms alone.

Most people now live somewhat removed from the necessity of having a fortress. Yet we do have various measures for keeping our homes safe. In my family growing up we used to joke that our house was like Fort Knox once my dad finished the evening lockup rounds. Some people have locks and bolts on everything, motion-sensing lights, and a state-of-the-art alarm system that, in case of unauthorized entry, would notify the security company, the police, the fire station, and probably mobilize the national guard.

Leaving aside suburbia for a moment, think of a fortress like Helm's Deep in J. R. R. Tolkien's *The Two Towers*:

> At Helm's Gate, before the mouth of the Deep, there
> was a heel of rock thrust outward by the northern cliff.
> There upon its spur stood high walls of ancient stone,
> and within them was a lofty tower. Men said that in
> the far-off days of the glory of Gondor the sea-kings
> had built here this fastness with the hands of giants.[4]

When the Bible says "refuge" or "fortress," we must picture a "fastness" with walls of high, thick, unbreachable stone.

God is our castle. My children have one of those books with detailed drawings of the inside of a medieval castle. The land around the castle is often depicted with gardens and fields and streams because the business of everyday life for the people took place outside the castle walls. But when a threat arose, the castle was there for them as a refuge. As it says in Proverbs 18:10, "The name of the LORD is a strong tower; the righteous man runs into it and is safe." The name of the Lord is his *identity*; it stands for all that we know him to be. Literally, we hide in *who* our God is.

---

4 Tolkien, *The Two Towers*, 143.

However encouraging this reminder is, the idea that God is our refuge isn't a novel one for most Christians. The challenge arises when we try to apply this truth to our fearful state. How can this help me in any sort of practical way when I'm fearful? For me, there has been more to it than merely intellectually accepting that God is a refuge. I have come to realize that hanging our trust on God means knowing not just who God is but who he has shown himself to be to me. Therein lies the power. We need not just a general faith in God but an *appropriating* faith.

Reading Spurgeon's comprehensive collection on the Psalms, I came across a story written by a Puritan named Fountain Elwin. He wrote,

> Suppose a traveler upon a bleak and exposed heath to
> be alarmed by the approach of a storm. He looks out
> for shelter. But if his eye discern a place to hide him
> from the storm, does he stand still and say, "I see there
> *is* a shelter, and therefore I may remain where I am?"
> Does he not betake himself to it? Does he not run in
> order to escape the stormy wind and tempest? It was
> a "hiding-place" before; but it was *his* hiding place
> only when he ran into it, and was safe. Had he not
> gone into it, though it might have been a protection to
> thousand other travelers who resorted there, to him it
> would have been as if no such place existed.[5]

God the fortress is there ... but we have to run into him! We have to make him our own like I made that random yellow house my own when I was nine years old. Where the rubber meets the road for our faith is when we claim refuge in God *as our own*. Not only is God called a refuge, fortress, stronghold, shield, and rock, but he is called *my* refuge, *my* fortress, *my* stronghold, *my* shield, and *my* rock.

5 See Spurgeon, *Treasury of David*, 1:96.

God doesn't represent *a* hiding place if only we can find it. He is *our* hiding place. I once counted 189 times in which personal possessive pronouns are used for God (or words referring to God, such as "refuge") in the Psalms alone.

This is where the beauty of the gospel comes in. This is the importance of what Paul called "the mystery of Christ"—that the gentiles can be "fellow heirs, members of the same body, and partakers of the promise in Christ Jesus through the gospel" (Eph 3:6). We have access to the God of the psalms and all his promises when we come to know Christ Jesus as Lord. He was not only a refuge for ancient Israel; he is our refuge, too.

For the last several years, I have had the privilege of meeting weekly with a dear friend from another culture to read the Bible. My friend comes from an atheistic background, and the only worship that went on in her home was ancestor worship, a feature of Confucianism. But her children were studying at a Christian school, and her desire for their academic success eventually interested her in knowing more about the Bible. We have been reading and discussing the Gospel of John, and it has been one of the best ongoing conversations of my entire life. My friend is intelligent, curious, honest, and reflective, and she comes to the life of Jesus as an entirely new experience. Through her incredulous eyes, I see the puzzling, miraculous story that it is all over again.

Over the months I watched my friend move from certainty that there was no God to a place of understanding the idea of a mighty, Creator God who had made all the world. We kept reading, and I kept waiting for God to touch her life. When we reached John 12 and read the story of Jesus's triumphal entry into Jerusalem, I asked her what she was thinking. "I think I am like one of those people standing in the crowd," she said. "Mary and Martha believed Jesus was God because he had just brought their brother back from the dead. But the people in the crowd don't know what to think about him. Because he didn't do anything for them. Maybe he is God or God's son. But he is not their God." I think my friend can now theoretically accept the truth of the

God of the Bible. But he isn't yet her God. She hasn't claimed him with the appropriation of personal faith.

My friend wants me to pray for her every time we meet, particularly when something concerning is happening. When her house helper told her there were ghosts in her house, she asked me to pray for her. I prayed for protection over her house in Jesus's name. The next week she was told that the ghosts were gone. When her husband had health problems and had to pursue treatment in his home country, she asked me to pray. When both of our sons were accidentally exposed to tuberculosis by their kindergarten teacher, a real threat in this country, she asked me to pray for protection over her son. "I know God will listen to you when you pray," she always says. "Because you know God, and he knows you." She recognizes that somehow I have a claim on God, that he will hear me when I pray to him.

Do you have a claim on God? Is the refuge he offers your own? If you have heard and understood the gospel, if you have repented of your sin and found the forgiveness available to you in God's Son Jesus Christ, if you have received the Holy Spirit by faith, then God is *your* God and therefore God is your castle when you are afraid. If we doubt that God is a valid refuge for us, if we think that he can't or won't keep us safe, what we are calling into question is nothing less than what Jesus won for us on the cross. Did he make us God's own once and for all, despite what we were, or did he not?

How does knowing God is your refuge give you any practical help when you're afraid? When you're afraid, dwell in God's protection. Remind yourself that he isn't just a refuge, he's *your* refuge. We should look at where the authors of the Bible looked when they were afraid. Let me offer some practical help drawn from two psalms. Psalms 48 and 62 employ the image of God as our refuge and provide useful examples of how to apply this truth when fears rise.

The first help comes from Psalm 48. This psalm states that "within [Zion's] citadels God has made himself known as a fortress" (v. 3). A fortress, according to Kidner's commentary on the Psalms, implies "a refuge set high up."[6] There is a multiplicity of closely related, overlapping terms applied to God in the Psalms: he is our refuge, our fortress, our rock, our shelter. These terms suggest that God is our source of strength, stability, protection, and confidence. While this psalm begins by identifying God as Zion's fortress, let me direct your attention to the end of the psalm:

> Walk about Zion, go around her,
>> number her towers,
>
> consider well her ramparts,
>> go through her citadels,
>
> that you may tell the next generation that this is God,
>
> our God forever and ever.
>> He will guide us forever. (vv. 12–14)

The psalmist seems to be instructing his listeners to make an architectural inspection of Jerusalem. We assume the purpose is to delineate the city's greatness. Yet after the walk and the count, the message the people are to proclaim is clear: "That you may tell the next generation that *this is God, our God* forever and ever. He will guide us forever" (vv. 13–14). In other words, God is inviting them to inspect their earthly city and draw spiritual analogies to his character—to what he is like as a fortress for them. It is not that the godly are to revel in the glories of the palaces of Jerusalem—they are to revel in the glory of God as thick walls and a roof! As John Calvin wrote, "By the aid of these outward things they should elevate their minds to the contemplation of the glory of God."[7]

---

6 Kidner, *Psalms 1–72*, 239.

7 Calvin, *Book of Psalms*, 2:232–33.

Sacred Courage

In Indonesia we have only two seasons: raining and not raining. The rainy season here frequently has rain that I had experienced only a few times in my life elsewhere. Suddenly the heavens will just split open with a roar, and water will crash down in a torrent, sheets of it blowing back and forth in the winds. Roads become rivers and anything not under cover is instantly and completely saturated. No one ever tries to "run between raindrops." Roofs here are made of tile or aluminum, and the rains rattling down on them produces a terrific din. I have stood at my front door, like at the mouth of a cave, and looked at the street in front of my house. It is like peering through a waterfall. We have also been walking through the rice paddies with our children, far from cover, when a downpour suddenly hit. Four walls and a roof take on new meaning at times like that. There is a curious exhilaration that comes from being tucked up inside with a terrific storm blasting around the house.

When we are amid such experiences, we need to note the sturdy walls, the lines of the roof over our heads, the sealed windows and doors. We should meditate on our physical safe space and map out the architecture of our refuge. Then, we must turn our thoughts to our God. *This* is what he is for us. *This* is what it feels like to take refuge in him. *This* is what he promises to be for us when disaster strikes. The people of God weren't instructed to count Jerusalem's towers and note the strength of its walls only so that they could broadcast the greatness of the city. More important than that, they would gain a clearer picture of the nature of their God. Throughout the Bible, God invites us to convert earthly experiences of safety and protection into spiritual reflection. In this way we can strengthen our appropriating faith.

And not only our own! As we engage in this spiritual discipline, we can also encourage this habit in our children and believers around us. Notice the connection in verse 13: "That you may tell the next generation that this is God, our God forever and ever." As we realize and revel in the safe structure that God is all around us, and tell our children or others about it, we will all be lifted into a more profound contemplation of the greatness of our God. (Indeed, as we will see in chapter 11, this is one of the ways we should be encouraging one another during these fearsome times.)

Now consider a few verses from Psalm 62, our second "refuge psalm" to help us in our battles with fear:

> For God alone, O my soul, wait in silence,
>> for my hope is from him.
>
> He only is my rock and my salvation,
>> my fortress; I shall not be shaken.
>
> On God rests my salvation and my glory;
>> my mighty rock, my refuge is God.
>
> Trust in him at all times, O people;
>> pour out your heart before him;
>> God is a refuge for us. Selah. (vv. 5–8)

In these verses we learn a few more concrete things we can do. First, the psalmist encourages his soul to "wait in silence." Actually, this passage both opens and closes by exhorting us to silence, because the word *selah* probably indicates some kind of pause or interlude for meditation.

O the priceless treasure that is silence! The value I place on it has grown immensely as the years of my life pass. I am so thankful to be a mother of four little people, and happy, noisy chaos has its charms, but sometimes I think I haven't heard what quiet sounds like in twelve years. I am so thankful to live on Java, but sometimes I feel like I can hear all 141 million people on this island. As I write this I am away from the children, but I can hear roosters crowing, mosques blasting the midday call to prayer, motorcycles revving on all sides, men talking, and children yelling.

I dream about the north woods of Minnesota on a calm day in winter, when the snow deadens all sound and one can stop trekking and stand motionless among the birch trees and hear absolutely nothing at all. Anne Morrow Lindbergh, in her little contemplative book *Gift from the Sea*, writes that the times of silence "are among the most important times in one's life—when one is alone.... . This is an end toward which we could strive—to be the still axis within the revolving wheel of relationships, obligations, and activities."[8]

The silence the psalmist commends is not an empty one. His silence was a waiting upon God. He "fills his thoughts with God" in the verses following.[9] Look at all the metaphors for God that David uses: God is our rock, our fortress, our refuge. He is also the source of our hope, salvation, and glory. David is buttressing his soul from different angles, piling up these truths against his soul's anxieties. We must not neglect the times of waiting on God, quieting the fearful clamor in our souls, and waiting silently for him to renew our hope.

In chapter 6 we saw that God has taken us into his confidence, making us his friends at the price of the cross. Here in Psalm 62, part of making God our refuge is that we must take God into our confidence too. This is what we are exhorted to do in response to God as our fortress, rock, and refuge. David urges, "Trust in him at all times, O people; pour out your heart before him; God is a refuge for us" (v. 8).

We are invited, even commanded, to give our innermost feelings and fears to God. We make him our refuge by entrusting to him the mixed contents of our hearts. When is the last time you really opened the storehouse of your soul to him? Let me just say here, this is an actual action. Thinking to ourselves that God cares about our fears, anxieties, and burdens, deciding that because he's God he must know everything already anyways, and skipping it and moving on to the next frantic activity is not pouring out our hearts before him. That is not an appropriating faith. There's no fast-forward button on opening our hearts to God.

8 Lindbergh, *Gift from the Sea*, 44.
9 Kidner, *Psalms 1–72*, 240.

What is the first thing many Christians say right after they urge you to pour out your heart to God? "He already knows your heart anyway." Of course he does. But God asks you to take an actual step of trust by pouring it out to him yourself. Think about it: When a close friend pours out her heart to me, should I respond, "I knew all that about you already"? Isn't it true that by confiding in me that friend has demonstrated her trust in me in a way that deepens and advances our relationship to one another? This dynamic is also present in our relationship with God.

So why is it not a contradiction to say "Wait for God in silence" and "Pour out your heart before him" in the span of four verses? These actions work together, not against each other. Try pouring out your heart to God with your phone in one hand and a baby in the other while frying meatballs and telling a toddler not to stand on the coffee table. You'll see what I mean. In order to pour out our hearts even to a human friend we must make time and space for the conversation. We have to seek that place of silence before God, and in that space, we are invited by him to pour out our hearts. They can be alternating activities—we pour, we wait, we pour, we wait. That is how we claim *our* God as *our* refuge.

Finally, the psalm says, "Trust him at all times." Of course, the hardest times to trust God are in the hardest times. It is easier in happier seasons, but how can we know in such times whether we are prepared to trust him as a refuge or not? I used to wonder, on steadier days, how would I react if a heavy grief or a momentous crisis hit me. If something terrifying suddenly happened, what would I do? I've imagined myself in circumstances like that. How would I handle it? Not just "what if" but "what would I do or say ... if?" Many of you have faced bigger crises than having a stroke, but that one was big for me and so I found out.

It's funny, in all the time I had wondered about it, it never occurred to me that I was asking the wrong question. Turns out it wasn't about my reactions at all. I was a hot mess all over the place, but that no longer seems important. The question I should have been asking—and answering for myself—is, What would God do? What will he do and say when my crises come? That's the answer that matters the most. He was—and is—a refuge. He is where our security lies. We must teach our souls the strength of this fortress.

Discussion Questions

1. Have you ever had the experience of seeking out a shelter for safety? How would you describe your emotional state before and after you found refuge?

2. How would you explain the difference between knowing that God is a refuge and knowing God as your refuge?

3. Is silence a part of your pursuit of God? What would it say about us if we rarely, if ever, poured out our hearts before God?

8

What about the Tricky Will of God?

> When Melancthon was extremely solicitous about the affairs of the Church in his days, Luther would have him admonished in these terms, "Monendus est Philippus ut desinat esse rector mundi": Let not Phillip make himself any longer governor of the world.
>
> —David Clarkson

Every night when our children are about to go to bed, they ask us to pray that they will have good dreams. It has become a crucial part of the nighttime routine that is never skipped, even if teeth don't get brushed or feet scrubbed (an important part of bedtime in Indonesia). The children rely on these prayers to ward off bedtime anxieties; they turn to them as a protection against fearing the night. They do this because this is what we have taught them from the beginning, when bedtime fears first reared from the shadows like a many-headed monster. We would offer prayer to Jesus as the only needed response. To this day they usually take it for granted that this will be enough to cover them for the night.

At one point, a few years ago, I noticed that our son Hugh's prayer had changed from a request for good dreams to asking God for no dreams at all.

"Why are you asking that you won't have any dreams at all?" I asked him. "Why not ask for good dreams?"

He responded, "What if God gives me a dream that he thinks is a good dream, but I don't like it? It's better to say no dreams at all."

He already knew at five years old that God's will might not line up with his own idea of what is good. He was certain in his utterly human little heart that only his own idea could be trusted.

In the previous chapter we looked at how God is our refuge. When we are afraid it helps us to claim our God, to take shelter in his name and his character, as in a strong tower. This does and should comfort us. But what questions or conflicts arise in your soul when you try to instruct it to fear God and take refuge in him?

I'll explain the conflict in my soul: when I try to find comfort in who God is, I run into an initial problem precisely *because* of who God is. God, you see, is God. Because he is God, I have no idea what he is really going to do in the circumstances of my life. Have you realized how scary that is? Hugh understood the crux of the matter with incredible clarity: What if God's idea of a good dream and my idea of a good dream are not the same? When it comes to facing off between what I want and what the sovereign God wants, I know which one won't happen.

This conflict in my soul has become greater, not less, the more I learn about God's total sovereignty in all things. "Our God is in the heavens; he does all that he pleases" (Ps 115:3). If God formed outer space, he is huge; if he said a word and the sun appeared, he is beyond all comprehension and powerful; if he knows everything, his wisdom makes all the libraries in the world (and the internet) ridiculous. All outcomes are determined by him. "The lot is cast into the lap, but its every decision is from the LORD" (Prov 16:33). Job said of the Lord, "I know that you can do all things, and that no purpose of yours can be thwarted" (42:2). If we let the Bible define for us the nature of God, it is undeniable and inescapable that not only does he bring all things about, but he planned them from the beginning. The problem is we don't understand why he does all that he does, and we cannot know what he will do next.

Oh, the tricky will of God! His thoughts and his ways are not ours, and they are as much higher than ours as the heavens are above the earth (Isa 55:8–9). To us, he's uncontainable, unpredictable, unfathomable. "How unsearchable are his judgments and how inscrutable his ways!" (Rom 11:33). We make a big mistake when we think we could fully explain his actions or his nature with our supposedly consistent logical systems. Though he has revealed himself to us in the Bible and in his Son Jesus Christ, much remains unknown.

When we Christians share our fears, a common response we offer as solace is, "God won't let that happen." Are you sure about that? Do we really know what God will do? This has to be a false idea of God because he *does* bring the things that we fear to some believers, and we know it. Telling ourselves, from our position of ignorance, that God won't do a certain thing isn't what it means to take refuge in God.

I fear that one of my children will have cancer. You can't tell me that God won't let that happen. He let it happen to several friends of mine—he could bring it to me and I know it. Another version of this statement is even worse: "God would never let that happen—not to a good person like me." This one combines a false idea of God with a false idea of me!

The way that fearing God and making him our refuge helps us is not that by doing so we somehow gain for ourselves a life with no threats and no danger. Fearing God isn't a guarantee; making him our refuge isn't a transaction. We do not thereby earn his favor, resulting in a better or easier earthly life. Look at Job, who is described multiple times as one who feared God and turned away from evil (1:1, 8; 2:3). Job had occasion to say, "The thing that I fear comes upon me, and what I dread befalls me" (3:25).

I wrote in chapter 4 that I suddenly had a stroke at age thirty-eight. In the days that followed, as we navigated through hospitals, medical tests, the complications of being overseas, and everybody's emotions and upheaval, it was hard for me to understand my own feelings. Finally, a week or two afterward, sitting alone in a hospital in Singapore, it came to me: my feelings were hurt. I felt exactly like God had slapped me. The question was there: How could God do that, and how could he do that to me? Don't give me that stuff about "God doesn't want bad things to happen, but sometimes he has to allow it." The point is that he could have stopped it, and he didn't. He could have made a different plan, but he made this one. He reminded me in a powerful, tangible, physical way that "the heart of man plans his way, but the LORD establishes his steps" (Prov 16:9).

This is why fear and control have such a close relationship. I want to direct my steps. I can count on what I can control. If I determine outcomes, they will never be what I don't want them to be. We "control freaks" are really just fearful people. We're protecting everyone and everything from an undesirable result. The hardest reality that we encounter is that we cannot determine what will happen to us and our loved ones. So it turns out that our battle with fear isn't just a battle with fear. It's a battle with our own need to be in control. Ultimately, we are not struggling with scary realities but wrestling with God himself. We are like Jacob who, afraid for his life, ends up not fighting with Esau but wrestling with the angel of God. "Bless me!" Jacob has the effrontery to demand (Gen 32:26). Aren't we often asking the same? How many of our prayers are versions of Jacob's cry? The struggle of Jacob is not unfamiliar to our own. It's the only battle we fight where in order to win we must surrender.

Randy Alcorn, in his book *If God Is Good: Faith in the Midst of Suffering and Evil*, wrote: "Your state of mind determines whether the doctrine of God's sovereignty comforts you or threatens you."[1] What must our state of mind be to find God's sovereignty comforting? What must we believe in order to relax at the prospect of outcomes uncontrolled by us? There are two crucial things we must accept that must impel our posture before God.

First, we must understand our true position in relation to God. The Old Testament repeatedly offers a particular metaphor for our existence in relation to God's sovereignty: we are like clay in his hands.

---

1 Alcorn, *If God Is Good*, 234.

Once God sent the prophet Jeremiah on a field trip to see how this works for himself.

> The word that came to Jeremiah from the LORD:
> "Arise, and go down to the potter's house, and there
> I will let you hear my words." So I went down to the
> potter's house, and there he was working at his wheel.
> And the vessel he was making of clay was spoiled in
> the potter's hand, and he reworked it into another
> vessel, as it seemed good to the potter to do. Then the
> word of the LORD came to me: "O house of Israel, can
> I not do with you as this potter has done? declares the
> LORD. Behold, like the clay in the potter's hand, so are
> you in my hand, O house of Israel." (18:1–6)

God wanted Jeremiah to be in the potter's actual house and see for himself the position of God's people: they are a lump of clay on the wheel, motionless unless the potter spins the wheel and forms the clay with his hands. The potter sits above, hands on the clay, doing the shaping. He formed the clay into a vessel as "it seemed good to the potter to do" (18:4). He is in the midst of the creative process, and the clay hasn't yet taken its final, finished form.

God gave us the same metaphor again through the prophet Isaiah:

> "Woe to him who strives with him who formed him,
>   a pot among earthen pots!
>
> Does the clay say to him who forms it, 'What are you
>   making?' or 'Your work has no handles'?
>
> Woe to him who says to a father, 'What are you begetting?'
>   or to a woman, 'With what are you in labor?'"
>
> Thus says the LORD,
>   the Holy One of Israel, and the one who formed him:

"Ask me of things to come;
  will you command me concerning my children and the
  work of my hands?
I made the earth
  and created man on it;
it was my hands that stretched out the heavens,
  and I commanded all their host." (45:9–12)

This is interesting. Does a lump of clay suddenly ask the potter what he's up to? Does it criticize the work in progress? Does it make alterations to the artist's plans? Of course not. It's clay. What we call artistic license belongs to the potter, not to the clay. As my husband once said in a sermon, "There are no advocacy groups for the rights of clay, arguing for what the clay wants to become." That would be a profound mistake. The same categorical difference that exists between the clay and potter exists between us and God.

We must acknowledge and accept the simple biblical truth that God is the potter. "But now, O LORD, you are our Father; we are the clay, and you are our potter, we are all the work of your hand" (Isa 64:8). By choosing to accept our proper position as clay, we accept that we are not always in a position to understand or approve of the potter's decisions.

Have you ever heard someone say "Because I said so" to a child? Perhaps the child keeps asking why he must do something or why his parent has made a particular decision. He is not answered by being invited to consider and evaluate the parent's reasons; he is answered with the parent's position of authority. It is really "Because I said so *and I am the Mommy.*" Parents do not always need or want to give their rationale.

These verses are like God's definitive "Because I said so." He said so and he is God. "Be still, and know that I am God," his voice says in Psalm 46:10 (a psalm subtitled "God is our fortress"). Many of us know this psalm for its encouragement that God is our refuge—"God is our refuge and strength, a very present help in trouble" (v. 1). But the conclusion that the author is working toward in verse 10, to be still and know that God is God, shows that he was asking the same questions about God that we are.

Even so, his final statement leaves no doubt that the need to be silent in the face of what God determines in no way means that he cannot find God to be a refuge: "The LORD of hosts is with us; the God of Jacob is our fortress" (46:11). The same attitude of silence is modeled for us by David in Psalm 39:9. He writes, "I am mute, I do not open my mouth, for it is you [LORD] who have done it." (I read this particular psalm in a different way than I used to do because this verse is followed by the words, "remove your *stroke* from me"!)

In the hospital in Singapore, one of my doctors gave me words of advice after my stroke. He said he was a medical professional but also a Christian. "In the days to come you will have many questions," he said. "But sometimes in life, the question we ought to be asking is not the question why." Perhaps we ought not ask it, but we still do. I even think it's okay to ask it. It's often part of the pouring out of our hearts that we looked at in chapter 7. It's okay as long as we recognize God doesn't owe us an answer.

So after we accept that God is the potter and we are the clay, what else must we do? The second thing we must do is endeavor to submit to God's will and surrender our own desires for our lives to him. The only real security is when God's will and my will are the same. This would be easily achieved should God's will happen to align with my own plans. But it is hard won when, by God's grace, I begin to conform my will to his plans. "We may have our own will," Charles Spurgeon wrote, "when our will is God's will."[2]

Yet we've just noticed how different God's will is from ours! We've just looked at how far beyond our control it is, how unpredictable it can be, how frankly unpalatable it can be. We've said God can and does bring hard and scary things sometimes. How on earth can we get to a place where we can surrender our will and desires for our lives fully to him? How could we ever trust him that much?

---

2 Spurgeon, *Treasury of David*, 1:301.

We are helped in this, as in all things, by Jesus. He stepped into human form not only to secure our friendship with God but to model for us how to submit to God's will. From the beginning, Jesus declared his purpose was to do God's will. He said things like, "I seek not my own will but the will of him who sent me" (John 5:30). He consistently attributes his actions to following the will of God. "For the works that *the Father has given me to accomplish*, the very works that I am doing, bear witness about me that the Father has sent me" (John 5:36). His summary of his earthly life was this: "I glorified you on earth, having accomplished the work that you gave me to do" (John 17:4). Jesus so fully embraced his purpose of fulfilling God's will that he was obedient "to the point of death, even death on a cross" (Phil 2:8).

At the moment of Jesus's ultimate submission of himself in death, we read about him in the garden of Gethsemane. Jesus knows he is to be arrested soon; he has a clear idea of what will follow that. He had told his followers on the way to Jerusalem just days before, "The Son of Man will be delivered over to the chief priests and the scribes, and they will condemn him to death and deliver him over to the Gentiles. And they will mock him and spit on him, and flog him and kill him" (Mark 10:33–34). Jesus knew what he was facing.

> And he took with him Peter and James and John,
> and began to be greatly distressed and troubled. And
> he said to them, "My soul is very sorrowful, even to
> death. Remain here and watch." And going a little
> farther, he fell on the ground and prayed that, if it
> were possible, the hour might pass from him. And
> he said, "Abba, Father, all things are possible for you.
> Remove this cup from me. Yet not what I will, but
> what you will." (Mark 14:33–36)

Both Matthew and Mark tell us that this prayer for the cup of suffering to be removed from him was prayed by Jesus three times in succession. Of everything possible that he could have been doing on the last night before his crucifixion, Jesus spent it wrestling with the will of God.

I was an adult before I realized that Jesus didn't want to die. I have never heard that idea in a sermon, and I don't remember anyone ever teaching it in Sunday school. But prone on the ground at Gethsemane Jesus pleaded with God to have a different plan. He wasn't just mouthing the words to set up a model for us, either. He meant it. We know he did because he repeated it over and over.[3] He fell to the ground, and as Luke reports, "Being in agony he prayed more earnestly; and his sweat became like great drops of blood falling down on the ground" (22:44). The first blood Jesus shed for us was the blood of his wrestling with God's will.

Despite voicing his desires to the contrary, he steps forward in obedience to God's will. Immediately after Jesus prays "Yet not my will but your will," armed soldiers flood the garden, and Jesus facilitates his own arrest. John tells us, "Then Jesus, knowing all that would happen to him, came forward and said to them, 'Whom do you seek?' And they said, 'Jesus of Nazareth.' Jesus said to them, 'I am he'" (18:4–5).

When Peter draws his sword and slices at the members of the detachment that came to Gethsemane to arrest Jesus, Jesus says to Peter, "Put your sword into its sheath; shall I not drink the cup that the Father has given me?" (18:11). Make no mistake, "the cup which was put to his lips was bitter: none of its bitterness was lost to him as he drank it: but he drank it; and he drank it *as his own* cup which it was his own will (because it was his Father's will) to drink."[4] When it comes to surrendering to God's will, Jesus is our ultimate example.

Interestingly, a significant proportion of the verses in the New Testament that instruct us to follow Jesus's example do so with reference to this aspect: Jesus surrendered to God's will and laid down his life for us. Peter wrote, "For to this you have been called, because Christ also

---

3 Matthew 26:42, 44; Mark 14:39, 41.

4 See Warfield, "The Emotional Life of our Lord," 134 *emphasis added*.

suffered for you, leaving you an example, so that you might follow in his steps" (1 Pet 2:21). Paul wrote, "Therefore be imitators of God, as beloved children; and walk in love, just as Christ also loved you and gave Himself up for us, an offering and a sacrifice to God as a fragrant aroma" (Eph 5:1–2 NASB). And Jesus himself said, "If anyone wishes to come after Me, he must deny himself, and take up his cross and follow Me" (Matt 16:24 NASB).

The author of Hebrews exhorts, "Let us run with endurance the race that is set before us, *looking to Jesus*, the founder and perfecter of our faith, who for the joy that was set before him endured the cross, despising the shame, and is seated at the right hand of the throne of God" (12:1–2). There we see again that Jesus did not want to go through the suffering of the cross—what we endure and despise is something that we don't want[5]—and that we are meant to look to his obedience as our example to follow.

Have you noticed that the words Jesus prays in Gethsemane, "Your will be done," echo what he instructed his disciples to pray in Matthew 6? He says, "Pray then like this: 'Our Father in heaven, hallowed be your name. Your kingdom come, your will be done, on earth as it is in heaven'" (6:9–10). He not only directly instructs us to pray like this, but he prays like this in the garden as he anticipates the cross. He sets up the principle, then he sets the example.

Sometimes when we try to think of Jesus as our example, we run into a roadblock. After all, he was God. We think that Jesus must have had an easier time because he was fully God as well as fully man. We think it was natural for Jesus to do the right thing because he was sinless. We want to put him into a different category. But Jesus came as a human in order to enter our category.

When Jesus came, he pitched his tent among us. He moved right into our neighborhood. When he put on humanity, he didn't put it on as one puts on clothes (and takes them off again). He didn't put it on as one puts on a play and enacts an imaginary scenario for a while. Jesus Christ

---

5 With thanks to Dr. Mark Talbot for helping me see this.

came in human form, and it became his very being. A man like no man ever. God in dirty sandals. When James wrote, "Draw near to God, and he will draw near to you" (4:8), he knew just how near God had already approached: God was his older brother.

Why did he do it? Was the most glorious form imaginable to the mastermind who crafted the solar system a human one? What in God's nature could best be communicated by the cosmic condescension of becoming as one of his own creatures?

The author of Hebrews didn't think that Jesus was disqualified as an example for us. Instead, he thought Jesus was *uniquely qualified* by his human experiences to represent us. He wrote,

> For we do not have a high priest who is unable to
> sympathize with our weaknesses, but one who in
> every respect has been tempted as we are, yet without
> sin. Let us then with confidence draw near to the
> throne of grace, that we may receive mercy and find
> grace to help in time of need. (4:15–16)

Jesus didn't come just as a symbolic human, a human archetype, or a human prototype. He came as a particular human being with emotions, desires, and personality traits. He was a man who knew that suffering awaited him and who did not want it—who wanted God to make a different plan. But he surrendered himself and his desires to God's will "for the *joy* that was set before him" (12:2).

So when our fears rise and we try to take refuge in God, we will realize that trusting God does not guarantee that the things we dread will not happen. The events we fear may transpire. But this book is not about how to keep suffering from happening or how to keep scary things at bay. (Too bad. That book would be a bestseller.) It is about how we face fear as the people of God. If we hope to achieve victory over fear in our lives, sooner or later we must recognize the sovereignty of God and surrender our will to his. As William Gurnall wrote, "Why should thou fear to be stripped of that which thou has resigned already to Christ?"[6] (In fact, our fears can be useful in showing us what we have not fully given to Christ.)

Do you want a stronger method of making God your refuge than just trusting he will never let any unwanted thing happen to you (but knowing that he might)? It is *surrendering* to God your refuge. James Burns puts this well:

> What is "resting in God" but the instinctive movement
> and upward glance of the spirit to him; the confiding
> of all one's griefs and fears to him, and feeling
> strengthened, patient, hopeful in the act of doing so!
> It implies a willingness that he should choose for us, a
> conviction that the ordering of all that concerns us is
> safer in his hands than in our own.[7]

The reason that fear has had such a stronghold in my own life is because I insist on retaining control; I have not sufficiently surrendered my desires to God. Yet when we are convinced that "the ordering of all that concerns us is safer in his hands than in our own," the stronghold of fear begins to come crumbling down. Submitting to the tricky will of God is a crucial aspect of our heart's victories against fear.

One of my most precious mentors was (and is) Elisabeth Elliot. It doesn't matter that we never met; she mentored me for years through her writing. My favorite nugget in all the gold of her writing is this one, though every time I read it, it knocks me over: "God is God. If he is God, he is worthy of my worship and my service. I will find rest nowhere but in his will, and that will is infinitely, immeasurably, unspeakably beyond my largest notions of what he is up to."[8]

---

6 William Gurnall, as quoted by Spurgeon, *Treasury of David*, 2:470.

7 James D. Burns, as quoted by Spurgeon, *Treasury of David*, 1:184.

8 Elliot, *Through Gates of Splendor*, epilogue.

Discussion Questions

1. When is it comforting to believe in God's sovereignty? When is it frightening?

2. Which areas of your life are the hardest to surrender to God? Where would you like to retain control?

3. How does Jesus help?

9

The Love of God

Could we with ink the ocean fill,
And were the skies of parchment made;
Were every stalk on earth a quill,
And every man a scribe by trade;
To write the love of God above
Would drain the ocean dry;
Nor could the scroll contain the whole,
Though stretched from sky to sky.

—Meir Ben Isaac Nehoraim (1050)

Despite many medical tests at an excellent hospital in Singapore, the doctors there did not discover the cause of my stroke. They could not explain why an otherwise healthy thirty-eight-year-old should suddenly develop the blood clot that struck my brain. In the end they labeled it "cryptogenic," which is medical jargon for "we have no clue." So they put me on a blood thinner and reluctantly released me to return to Indonesia. But the blood thinners are risky for a person living in a developing country, removed from good medical care. We also suspected that the medication was making me feel even worse.

Finally, we had to return to the United States, where God provided an opportunity to see a neurologist who found the reason for the stroke: I have fibromuscular dysplasia (FMD). FMD is a condition of unusual cellular growth in the arteries. This can lead to weakness of the artery walls, leaving them vulnerable to tearing. If they tear, a blood clot can form that eventually releases into the bloodstream and, being carried to the brain, causes a stroke. We don't know what caused the disease, how long I've had it, or if it will get worse. There isn't a treatment except taking blood thinners to reduce the risk of clots. One doctor also suggested that I avoid skydiving, rollercoasters, and high-impact sports. No problem.

Sacred Courage

The nut in all this shell is that no one could promise me that I wouldn't have another stroke. Because it is dangerous to live in Indonesia on a heavy-duty blood thinner, the doctors suggested I take an aspirin every day to reduce the risk of clots. One doctor told me confidently that the aspirin would reduce my risk of another stroke "by about 70 percent." Their guesses were all statistics and likelihoods. I told you in chapter 2 how profoundly unhelpful I find these when I am afraid. The one question I wanted answered was how to make certain I would not have another stroke, and that's the answer I did not get. Basically, they don't know.

I have never been so mad at God in my entire life.

Let me recap for you. Up until then, my life had been unfolding roughly according to plan. By God's miraculous grace alone we had progressed through the turmoil of the transition to Indonesia. I believed I had finally achieved some victory over fear in my life; I was feeling stable, even encouraging my husband to travel. Then God struck me down on my family room floor. Not only was I left with trauma and brain damage, but I was plunged right back into the morass of worries and anxieties as fear not only reappeared in my life but appeared in ways I had never experienced before. Then I found out I have a disorder that means this can happen to me again at any time—and there's nothing that can be done about it. I am beyond what medicine can do (especially since returning to Indonesia). I don't know if my stroke story is over or if this is intermission. Only God does.

It just didn't make any *sense*. Why would God put me in this precarious position?

In the previous chapter I wrote about the conflict in my soul that can arise when I try to make God my refuge in fearful times. Then I realize that his will may not be my preference. This conflict has become greater, not less, as I learn more of God's total sovereignty. I know that he never promised that the things I am afraid of will not happen. I find that life as a lump of clay is scary. It is hard to live our lives in the garden of Gethsemane. But though surrendering to God's will is a crucial step in the fight of faith, it is not the only step.

Sometimes it seems like the more we get to know the character of our God, the more intimidating he becomes. Perhaps we theological types are in the most danger of this. In our pursuit of taking an honest look at who God is, we can emphasize certain traits in God's character in a way that throws the whole picture off-kilter. The sovereignty, the vastness, the power, and the holiness are all there and they make an incredibly intimidating total. But these traits are not the whole picture. We must try to see God clearly in *all* his attributes because how we see him is crucially important. A. W. Tozer begins his book *Knowledge of the Holy* with these words:

> What comes into our minds when we think about
> God is the most important thing about us ... the
> gravest question before the Church is always God
> Himself, and the most portentous fact about any man
> is not what he at a given time may say or do, but what
> he in his deep heart conceives God to be like. We tend
> by a secret law of the soul to move toward our mental
> image of God.[1]

Tozer helped me recognize that the central question underneath the battle with fear is really "What is our actual mental image of God?" Additionally, and just as important, "How do we picture God's posture toward us?" It hasn't been enough for me to realize the absolute sovereignty of God outside of and apart from me—what God is like in himself. What matters most is how I view God's character in relationship to me. Thus, the most portentous fact about any woman is what she in her deep heart conceives God to be like and how he views her.

We may think the solution to fear is trusting in a powerful God, one who is stronger than the things we fear and someone who can protect us. Yet I have become convinced that this conception of God must be supplemented with the mental image of a God of *love* who loves *me*. I've realized that the struggle I have had with fear all of my life is actually

---

1 Tozer, *Knowledge of the Holy*, 1.

just growing from the root struggle that I have had with accepting God's love. This has been a big missing piece in my understanding of God's character. I know that God's will is beyond my understanding and could—and will—include hard things ahead. This belief in God's sovereignty has overshadowed my view of God as a loving Father who is good and delights to be good to me.

Consider the book of Lamentations. Certainly, the author of this book recognized and submitted to the sovereignty of God. He writes this of Jerusalem: "Her foes have become the head; her enemies prosper, *because the LORD has afflicted her for the multitude of her transgressions*" (1:5). Again through the prophet's voice, Jerusalem laments, "Look and see if there is any sorrow like my sorrow, which was brought upon me, which the LORD inflicted on the day of his fierce anger" (1:12). The author of this book does not credit the Babylonians with the destruction of Jerusalem—this is God's doing. God has been the one in control the entire time.

Deuteronomy also warns Israel of the curses for disobedience to the covenant, curses that finally fell upon Judah in Jeremiah's day:

> And among these nations you shall find no respite,
> and there shall be no resting place for the sole of your
> foot, but the LORD will give you there a trembling
> heart and failing eyes and a languishing soul. Your
> life shall hang in doubt before you. Night and day you
> shall be in dread and have no assurance of your life. In
> the morning you shall say, "If only it were evening!"
> and at evening you shall say, "If only it were morning!"
> because of the dread that your heart shall feel.
> (Deut 28:65–67)

I have never experienced anything like the siege of Jerusalem or exile into a hostile nation, but I can relate to the feeling of dread, having no assurance of the circumstances of my life.

So how did the author of Lamentations deal with the dread, uncertainty, and despair of his situation? Was he comforted solely by reflecting on the sovereign will of God? The turning point in the book of Lamentations occurs when he recalls God's love.

> But this I call to mind,
> and therefore I have hope:
>
> The steadfast love of the LORD never ceases;
> his mercies never come to an end;
>
> they are new every morning;
> great is your faithfulness.
>
> "The LORD is my portion," says my soul,
> "therefore I will hope in him." (3:21–24)

The author is not in easy circumstances. He writes, "My soul is bereft of peace; I have forgotten what happiness is. So I say, 'My endurance has perished; so has my hope from the LORD'" (3:17–18). In that latter statement, he is talking to himself. Things are about as bad as they can be, and his inner monologue evidences both doubt and hopelessness. This is the time when fear becomes powerful in a believer's life. Of what are we afraid if not the kind of suffering and loss that the author experienced? Of what are we afraid if not that our hope in God won't pan out?

But then he begins to talk to himself at a deeper level—he's already said that his endurance and hope have perished, but what he's spoken over himself in the dark isn't the last word. He then calls to mind that his hope is pinned on the steady love and daily goodness of God (3:21–23). He's actively reminding himself. Look at his self-talk after this reminder: "'The LORD is my portion,' says my soul, 'therefore I will hope in him'" (3:24). Despite national failure and covenant-breaking, the author somehow held onto the steadfast covenant love of God. He was convinced that God was not done with his people.

L. M. Montgomery's beloved character Anne Shirley famously says, "Tomorrow is always fresh with no mistakes in it." But as soon as I get to tomorrow, there will be mistakes in it! How amazing to know that God has mercies waiting for us afresh when we wake up tomorrow morning. There's no interruption of his goodness, his gifts, or his love. It flows unceasingly from him to us, and on this we build our hope. Our lifelong portion is that God is present and merciful in every day that dawns, no matter how difficult, how scary, or even how ordinary it may seem. As Tish Harrison Warren wrote, "Each morning in those first tender moments—in simply being God's smelly, sleepy beloved—I again receive grace, life, and faith as a gift."[2] She writes about the struggle to train herself "to live with my eyes open to God's presence in this ordinary day."[3] The dailiness, the repetition of the Christian life, creates familiarity until even the most awesome truths can seem ordinary. But familiarity, in the case of the mercy and goodness of God, doesn't breed contempt. For us it breeds security.

When our fearful souls run to Jesus and our trembling inner selves feel the peace of God descending, it is *always* astonishing in its utterly unmerited bounty. The gracious peace, the flood of rest to the soul that the Spirit of God gives could never be overfamiliar—it's more reassuring, more comforting, more beautiful every single time. It's new every day, and it's better every day.

Friends, we stand on even more solid covenantal footing than the author of Lamentations did. We are members of a better covenant with greater hope and greater confidence. Perhaps it has been said many times, but nevertheless the answer to fear and all of our problems really is the gospel, the new covenant made by the blood of Christ and sealed

---

2 Warren, *Liturgy of the Ordinary*, 20.

3 Warren, 36.

by the Holy Spirit. The gospel of God's love addresses the wellspring of fear: our own hearts. When confronting our fear, we need to hear the gospel yet again.

When I was a chubby three-year-old, I prayed my first prayer to Jesus. I trusted him then in the same way that I trusted in everything my mother said. In the last forty years I have heard the gospel so many times. The presence of Jesus has been a steady force, an ever-brightening light, an ever-nearer intimacy. Except when it hasn't. There have been so many times when I've become encrusted with layers of apathy, when I've taken Jesus and his death on the cross for granted, when I've grown arrogant in my salvation. I've started to feel, at times, that my "testimony"—the tale of Christ in my life—was uninteresting. I would hear how God was waiting with mercy at the end of a runaway's road or the bottom of an addict's cycle, and I would think my story was undramatic, maybe a bit boring. I did not see the weighty mercy of having known him since I was a child.

I'll never forget the first time my oldest child, Norah, heard the story of the crucifixion at about three years old. And I'll never forget how unexpectedly hard it was for me to tell it. We were reading her children's Bible together, when she saw a picture of Jesus carrying a cross. "What is Jesus doing?" she asked. I stared down into her little blue eyes and it came crashing in on me that it is a horrible, violent story for a tiny girl. This was a tiny girl who thought some of the pages in the book *Baby Animals on the Farm* were scary and who couldn't bear to watch *Frosty the Snowman*. Suddenly, I saw the gospel story as a tale of betrayal, brutality, and blood. How could I tell her what they did to Jesus?

You see, I'd grown up with it. I was told about Jesus at such a young age and so frequently that I'd forgotten a few simple facts about the story of his life on earth. I'd forgotten, for example, how fantastic a tale it is. God became a man, lived on earth, and died on a cross to save humankind. He raised people from the dead, healed untreatable diseases, and walked on water. He calmed the storm. It's like pages out of a superhero comic book. I had also forgotten—or maybe I never realized—how gory it is. Jesus was unjustly accused and tortured to death. We can become numb to it because we've heard the phrases in which the story is told so many times that they have become cant. But the fact is, they shamed him, beat him, jabbed thorns into his head, and nailed his living body to a cross, on which he slowly suffocated to death. A human being. I hadn't seen it like that in so long. I don't know if I ever had.

There is a picture in *The Jesus Storybook Bible* that shows a cartoon Jesus up close on the cross, with a crude "Our King" sign nailed over his head. His wounds are represented with a few little slash lines, and there is a tiny tear on his cheek. It's simple, like the text that explains it: "They nailed Jesus to the cross." Slowly turning the pages, I told Norah how the soldiers took Jesus away from his friends. I said, "They gave him owies, Norah. And he died." She stared at the picture, her eyes enormous. "Jesus *died*?" Her daddy walked in just then and she called out, "Jesus had owies, Daddy! They gived Jesus owies. Him died!" She was astonished. She asked me over and over, double checking. After all, what she knew about Jesus was that he welcomed the children, helped the sick people, and loved Zacchaeus. Why would anyone want to hurt Jesus?

I know the cross is just the beginning of that story. But I found that I wanted to skip it, or skate quickly over it, and get to the happy ending. But she needed to know. So I told her they nailed the Son of God to a cross and he died there. I told her the soldiers rolled a big rock to shut his body in the dark tomb. When it was time for the good news, I tried to put all of the stunning delight of Easter morning into my voice and I said, "But *then* ..." And it struck me anew that the tomb was wide open, and his body wasn't there. For a long time afterward, I overheard Norah telling the story to her dolls or her baby sister, with the echoes of that "*then*" in her voice. "But *then* ... Jesus wasn't there! He's alive again! No more owies! He's okay! Here he is!"

Norah helped me see again what I had all but stopped seeing. Are we bringing the truth of the gospel, with its stunning good news of God's unmerited favor and unconditional love for us, to bear on our battle with fear? In all my wrestling and all my pondering what I've come to is this: Much of my struggle with fear is because I still need to grasp God's love for me. Perhaps that truth is familiar—yet so is oxygen. I need to breathe the love and goodness of God in all day like oxygen and live my life by the strength of it.

How can we do this? How can we ever fully accept the love of God? The answer is that we need spiritual power and strengthening. Paul's letter to the Ephesians describes it.

Before we reach Ephesians 3:14–19, which is where we're headed, let's put that passage into its context. The ancient city of Ephesus "had a reputation in antiquity as a place where magical practices flourished."[4] This type of environment is somewhat familiar to me as I live in a culture that is aware of spiritual forces and often resorts to amulets, spells, and black magic.

Paul's prayer in chapter 1 makes a lot of sense: as believers in a context of malignant powers we need to know "what is the immeasurable greatness of his power toward us who believe" (v. 19). Yet this is only Paul's initial prayer for the Ephesians, not his climactic one. Knowing God's power is the baseline for our fight against fear, not the pinnacle.

Muslims too believe in the absolute sovereignty of Allah. The idea of the power of God is not unfamiliar to them. Yet they often still fear the spirits and run to the witch doctor with their problems. I think the real issue is that there is no equivalent in their belief system to our understanding of the love of God and the gospel. They don't believe that God not only has the power to protect them but also the willingness—or the covenantal commitment in steadfast love—to work for their good.

Notice what follows after Paul's prayer in chapter 1. Chapter 2 is perhaps the most beautiful expression of the gospel in all the Bible. It

---

4 Arnold, *Ephesians*, 37.

explains how I as a gentile, as one who had no hope and was without God in the world, could find peace with God through the Messiah promised to the Jews.

Finally, then, we come to the well-known prayer in 3:14–19. Paul understood that our best weapon for fighting fear is the knowledge of the unshakeable love of Christ—for us. Perhaps Christian growth or maturity is just growing confidence in the love of God. Look at Paul's main prayer request for the Ephesian church:

> I pray that out of his glorious riches he may strengthen
> you with power through his Spirit in your inner being,
> so that Christ may dwell in your hearts through faith.
> And I pray that you, being rooted and established
> in love, may have power, together with all the Lord's
> holy people, to grasp how wide and long and high and
> deep is the love of Christ, and to know this love that
> surpasses knowledge—that you may be filled to the
> measure of all the fullness of God. (vv. 16–19 NIV)

Looks like we're not alone in needing to deepen our understanding of the love of Christ. This need forms the core of Paul's pastoral prayer. Make no mistake, grasping this love does not come naturally to us—it is the supernatural gift of strengthening and power of comprehension that only comes through the Spirit.

Sometimes Christians say that God sees us with a perpetual smile on his face. I find myself operating as though perhaps God smiles a little sometimes (when I earn it by doing something good). But I can't get away from a picture of alternating smiles and grimaces as God watches my life. I have struggled to fully believe in God's love for me. I can't rest in it. I can't imagine that he's not annoyed, disappointed, or even frustrated at my brokenness, sin, and failures. I recall the things I've done, the things I've said, the people I've hurt or disappointed, the people that have confronted or accused me, and I cringe. I conceive of God as another critic, only of course with even more information about who I really am. He knows how selfish, how materialistic, how hypocritical, and how shallow I am. How could he be smiling?

I can believe God's love for us as collective humanity on a general level: "For God so loved *the world* that he sent his only Son" (John 3:16). But I can't put merely my own name in that verse. It's as though subconsciously I think he died for the lump value of everybody else and I'm a lucky add-on. I have a hard time seeing God's love for me in particular.

Of course, I know that I need to believe the gospel: I can see how much God loves me in that he sent Jesus to die on the cross to save me. I realize that what I am doubting underneath all of this is nothing less than the efficacy of the cross of Christ to cover quite *all of my sin*. The faithful Christian life is perhaps just a cycle of believing, at ever-deepening levels of the human soul, the simple-not-easy truth of the gospel itself; of seeing how it applies to and transforms life's every new situation and every emotion. But the truth of it should shine brighter and brighter as it grows in familiarity—its impact should grow greater, not less.

A story is told about the great English painter J. M. W. Turner: "He is said to have been engaged upon one of his immortal works, and a lady of rank looking on remarked, 'But Mr. Turner, I do not see in nature all that you describe there.' 'Ah, Madam,' answered the painter, 'do you not wish you could?'"[5] Turner's pictures, particularly of natural phenomena such as light and air and water and storm, do not oversell the beauty that is really there. But the lady couldn't see it. She could see the colors in Turner's painting, but she could no longer spot them in the sky. She probably viewed a sunset as just a daily occurrence.

Have the colors of the gospel become a bit like a daily occurrence to us?

---

5 J. M. W. Turner, as quoted by Spurgeon, *Treasury of David*, 1:281.

Underneath my ongoing battle with fear is this deeper problem: I had stopped seeing the wonder of the gospel itself. I had stopped reacting to it as the incredible tale of undeserved, unconditional love that it is. The death of Jesus on the cross and his resurrection hold the central place in all of human life and experience and these realities reach relevantly into every corner of our lives and speak to every struggle that we have. But we forget it so easily. As Tish Harrison Warren writes in *Liturgy of the Ordinary*, "We have lost our capacity to see wonders where true wonders lie."[6]

Paul didn't just pray for the physical protection of the Ephesians, their moral purity, or their missional effectiveness. He prayed that the believers would be "rooted and established" in love, like trees firmly planted in good soil, to keep expanding their sense of being loved by God. I love that Christ strengthens us "through the Spirit in our inner being." He knows us from the inside out. He knows all that we are, all that we fear, and how much we don't deserve his love. Yet the love here described is so extensive—it is three-dimensional and vast to the point that it defies description ("surpasses knowledge" in Eph 3:19). God is intimately acquainted with our true selves and *yet* he loves us that much.

In the garden of Eden, before the world was broken, Adam and Eve lived in this idyllic state of being naked and unashamed (Gen 2:25). Ever since, through all the generations of fallen man, we have carried the guilt, the fear, and the shame. We could not get back to that perfect, restful state before God until Jesus came and reinvented "naked and unashamed" as "fully known and fully loved."

If we've understood what Jesus did for us on the cross and claimed it through faith, from there it's just a deep dive into a love in which we'll never find the bottom. Spurgeon wrote, "Futurity shall be but a continual development of the good things which the Lord has laid in store for us."[7] If we are continually deepening our understanding of the

---

6 Warren, *Liturgy of the Ordinary*, 34.

7 Spurgeon, *Treasury of David*, 1:175.

phenomenal love of Christ, we will also be continually discovering fresh examples of that love as our lives extend into eternity. Want to smile at the future like the Proverbs 31 woman? Imagine all the ways that Jesus waits to be good to you tomorrow. Like the line in Anna Letitia Waring's beautiful old hymn "My Heart is Resting, O My God": "Glory to thee for all the grace I have not tasted yet."[8]

He is smiling, he will work it all out for good, and he does—he really does—dearly love us. At long last, finally, *that* is fear's true antidote: the knowledge of the deep, deep love of Jesus. Jesus's love is wide and high and long and deep. It is, in fact, perfect.

And, my friends, perfect love casts out fear.

---

8 Waring, *Hymns and Meditations.*

Sacred Courage

Discussion Questions

1. Take a look inside. Do you think you really believe that God loves you?

2. At what times in your life have you felt God's particular love for you? At what times, or in what circumstances, has it been harder to believe?

3. What grace do you have to look forward to?

4. Of what can you be certain?

10

We Fall to the Level of Our Training

I am a creature of a day, passing through life as an arrow through the air. I am a spirit come from God, and returning to God: just hovering over the great gulf; til, a few moments hence, I am no more seen; I drop into an unchangeable eternity! I want to know one thing—the way to heaven; how to land safe on that happy shore. God himself has condescended to teach me the way. For this very end he came from heaven. He hath written it down in a book. O give me that book! At any price, give me the book of God! I have it: here is knowledge enough for me. Let me be *homo unius libri*—a person of one book.

—John Wesley

I learned to drive in Fargo, North Dakota. Our main competitors in high school sports were small schools in the surrounding rural communities. Driving to these places meant long, straight miles of open prairie where nothing could shield you from whatever the huge sky threw at you. For about seven months of the year, that was ice and snow. It was not unusual for people to be caught in sudden blizzards, buried under snowbanks in their cars. So, my father insisted that our cars include a winter survival kit for our safety. Packed into these were wool blankets, a flashlight, a tin can, matches, candles, flares, a rope, and a snow shovel. There was some intention of including energy bars, but somehow these always seemed to be missing. I remember Dad instructing us what to do if we were buried by a blizzard and stuck in the car in the open country: cocoon in the blankets for warmth and melt snow in the can for water. The rope could be used to exit the vehicle for a short distance without getting lost in the blizzard.

Sacred Courage

The whole point of carrying the survival kit in the car was that it would be there when you needed it. My dad had been a Boy Scout, and he had fully internalized their motto: Be prepared. When the winds begin to gust and the flurries swirl around, it's too late to pack the survival kit. It must be there ahead of time.

There is a spiritual survival kit that we need to pack *before* fear surges up in our souls. The battle with fear is often won or lost before it starts, depending on how we have readied our hearts. If we are scrambling for spiritual resources in the moment that fears gather like clouds before a storm, it is often too late. We will be left to cower and hope the storm will blow over, ill-equipped to stand strong in the blast. The time to prepare is on sunny days.

The spiritual survival kit we need is the truth of the word of God. It is prepared through the spiritual disciplines of Bible reading and prayer, those time-worn pillars of Christian practice upon which we build so much. It turns out they are of gravest importance in the fear battle. These vital practices are called "disciplines" for a reason—they provide the necessary training for our spiritual walk.

Undoubtedly, an exhortation to read the Bible and pray is conventional advice—not original or surprising. You will probably quickly realize that the basic message of this chapter is one you already know: strength and comfort, which we each need, are available in the pages of Scripture and the practice of prayer. Indeed, this has been the guiding principle of each chapter in this book. But is this advice so standard that we take it for granted—as though the help we need is hiding in plain sight? Have you read this book looking for some system or special technique to fortify your soul? Meanwhile, if fear is looming large in your life, could it be time for you to revive these disciplines?

I won't apologize for offering such basic advice. Every new generation of Christians needs these disciplines. They have to be the constant drumbeat in the rhythm of the church's life. We neglect them at our peril. I have shared about many seasons in my life when fear was my primary spiritual struggle. Truthfully, the times when fear seems to be winning are the times when I have been neglecting my Bible and prayer. Coincidence? I think not. God gave these vital practices for our spiritual survival; they are how we find help. As the author of Hebrews exhorts us, "Let us then with confidence draw near to the throne of grace, that we may receive mercy and find grace to help in time of need" (4:16). We do so through prayer and God's word. The great promise is that help is available.

We prepare our "fear survival kit" first by reading the Bible. The Bible is where we are meant to find hope in our struggles. As Paul wrote to the Romans, "For whatever was written in former days was written for our instruction, that through endurance and through the encouragement of the Scriptures we might have hope" (15:4).

Perhaps words don't seem like enough to arm yourself in the face of all we have to fear. On the scale of effectiveness, we tend to think of "just words" in a lower category than, say, decisive actions. (Remember the old playground chant? "Sticks and stones may break my bones, but words will never hurt me.") But words spoken by God are different. As God says to Job, "Have you an arm like God, and can you thunder with a voice like his?" (Job 40:9). God hung the sun with words (Gen 1:16). He told the sea where to stop with words (Ps 104:9; Job 38:11). The words of God are uniquely powerful, creative, and regenerative. It is in contact with just these words that our hearts are transformed.

The Scriptures are inhabited in a mysterious, indescribable way with the voice of God himself—he who breathed the world into being, breathed the word into being. And he's speaking to us still between the covers of our printed Bibles. As Paul wrote to Timothy, "All Scripture is *breathed out* by God and profitable for teaching, for reproof, for correction, and for training in righteousness, that the man of God may be complete, equipped for every good work" (2 Tim 3:16–17). I think they ought to publish a version that makes the sound of the wind when one lifts the cover to remind us every time we open it: Here blows the breath of God.

Together with reading God's word, we pack our survival kits through prayer. Because we can't see it, we profoundly underestimate the work that God is doing in our hearts and souls when we pray (not to mention our circumstances). When it comes to a particular fear or anxiety, can you really have "trusted the Lord" if you have not given it to him thoroughly in prayer? What does trusting him even mean if not that? And if we have not done so, why do we expect to be able to respond in faith and courage? In the words of Archilochus, an early Greek poet who was also probably a soldier, in a crisis "we don't rise to the level of our expectations, we fall to the level of our training." We need to practice taking to our knees until it becomes second nature.

I wonder, have we even begun to realize the One who is available to us through prayer? Our God has revealed himself to be profoundly personal; he has opened a line of direct communication with each of us. In Genesis, the desperate runaway Hagar, awed at being noticed by God, called him the "God of seeing" (16:13). We not only have a God who sees us, wondrous as that is, but also a God who *hears us*. He listens to what we say. David calls him "O you who hear prayer" (Ps 65:2). The God of hearing is available to us through prayer; the God who speaks is available to us through his written word. How we need to avail ourselves of these precious means that God has provided!

How then should we read our Bibles and pray when we're afraid? There's no magic method or secret formula; the mysterious way that the Bible and prayer shape us isn't even a process controlled or directed by us. Libraries of books have been written on the Scriptures and prayer, filled with insights far beyond the ken of this book and its author. So I simply want to suggest three ways to pursue these disciplines if we truly want fear to recede and if we are seeking a heart anchored and secured in the love of Christ.

First, we must read the Bible and pray daily. Before our Bibles were complete, God created a powerful metaphor for his word when he sent manna to the Israelites in the desert. In Deuteronomy 8:3, Moses clarified God's reason for sending it:

> And he humbled you and let you hunger and fed you
> with manna, which you did not know, nor did your
> fathers know, that he might make you know that man
> does not live by bread alone, but man lives by every
> word that comes from the mouth of the LORD.

Could God really have rained bread from the sky daily for decades just to symbolize the relationship he wants us to have with his word? Yes. Have another look at the details in Exodus 16. Everybody went out to gather it: "Gather of it, each one of you, as much as he can eat" (v. 16). No matter how much they gathered, they still ended up with just as much as each one needed to eat. "They gathered, some more, some less. But when they measured it with an omer, whoever gathered much had nothing left over, and whoever gathered little had no lack. Each of them gathered as much as he could eat" (vv. 17–18).

The manna that fell couldn't be saved. It fell fresh every morning and had to be gathered every day. Anything left over from the day before wasn't just a little dry or stale, it "bred worms and stank" (v. 20). But gathered daily, it tasted sweet: "It was like coriander seed, white, and the taste of it was like wafers made with honey" (v. 31). The manna sustained God's people for their entire journey through the desert and into the promised land. "The people of Israel ate the manna forty years, till they came to a habitable land. They ate the manna till they came to the border of the land of Canaan" (v. 35).

We each *individually* need the word of God to make it through this desert of vulnerable life on earth. We can't rely on what we've gathered in the past, what we already know, or what we've stored up in other seasons. We need it fresh daily as we trudge forward. And it is sweet.

Our daily need is the basis for the emphasis on the disciplines of daily Bible reading and prayer in the church. Of course, this isn't a new insight but an ancient practice. Yet I want to emphasize that this practice (and that of prayer) protects us from the onslaught of fear. We gather and eat each morning so that in the heat of the sun we will not wither with worry and anxiety.

Of course, the problem with any consistent, quotidian routine of this sort is that it becomes a mere duty. If you shut your eyes and I say "duty," what do you see? Taxes? Laundry? When did "duty" become a dirty word? When did it take on the same connotations as "burden"? Perhaps we see unpleasant things or get a nasty taste in our mouths from this word because in our world duties are suspect and passions are championed. Doing something only because we are "supposed to" is considered worse than not doing it at all. John Piper famously wrote in *Desiring God* about what would happen if he gave his wife roses and, when thanked, gave "It's my duty to love you" as a response.[1] He was right—she wouldn't like it. Yet that's a faithful man! It's true: he *ought* to do thoughtful and loving things for his wife (though it may not be the best policy to say so). Whenever the word *ought* was struck from our working vocabulary (for struck it has been) we lost something precious: a big, basic building block from the foundations of faithfulness.

Perhaps you don't see a problem with spiritual disciplines being a duty. For the Christian, our duties and our passions should lie together. But sometimes our passions float all over the place. Sometimes, though we love Jesus, waking up and studying our Bibles or focusing our minds to pray are the last things we feel passionate about. Duty is then what gets us there. Duty is like the garden trellis on which we train the vines of our passions as they grow Godward.

Duty and routine are crucial because we are made to be creatures of habit. This is turned to good account when the habits we build into

---

1 Piper, *Desiring God*, 93.

our lives are faithful ones. C. S. Lewis wrote, "When we carry out our 'religious duties' we are like people digging channels in a waterless land, in order that when at last water comes, it may find them ready."[2] Lewis was writing about waiting for renewal in dry times. But his insight could be rewritten to fit the present argument: When we carry out our "religious duties," we are like people who build walls in a dangerous land so that, when the attack finally comes, we may be ready.

Our Muslim friends understand the importance of habit well. During the recent world pandemic, when the COVID-19 virus began to spread rapidly in Indonesia, everything shut down and there was a national campaign of "Di rumah aja" ("Just stay at home"). The Muslim lady who helps us in our house didn't come to work for a couple of months. This was mostly as a protection for her—foreigners like us were considered to pose a health risk because the virus was seen as a "foreign" illness. Many weeks into the crisis, when our helper came to pick up her pay, I asked her how she was doing with the isolation. It wasn't until I mentioned that I knew the mosques were closed and she could not attend daily prayers that she began to cry. She told me that was the hardest thing. "Now, when we most need to gather and pray to Allah," she said, "we cannot do it." All her life, she has been used to turning to the routine practices of religion, rain or shine, literally as the day comes in and the day goes out.

This is why we have liturgy, whether we label it such or not. Liturgy is simply the forms and practices by which we worship God. These forms and practices are duties, but they are more than that. They are what make us who we are. Tish Harrison Warren has identified the formative nature of our daily habits: "Our hearts and our loves are shaped by what we do again and again and again."[3] I have heard that "fear is really desire turned on its head," meaning that all fear exists because we want certain

---

2 Lewis, *Reflections on the Psalms*, 113.
3 Warren, *Liturgy of the Ordinary*, 33.

things to happen (and worry they may not) and we do not want other things to happen (and worry they may). If this is true, then the things our hearts desire dictate what our fears will be. Thus, what we want and our hearts truly love and desire is critically important in shaping us as unafraid people of God.

In short, our desires must be reformed so that we want what God wants. As James K. A. Smith wrote in *You Are What You Love*, "The practices of Christian worship train our love—they are practice for the coming kingdom, habituating us as citizens in the kingdom of God. Christian worship ... is essentially a *counter*formation to those rival liturgies we are often immersed in."[4] The news, Facebook, and Twitter are powerful "rival liturgies"! They make us afraid. But the Bible, as we read it daily, will make us strong in the Lord.

Not only must we read the Scriptures daily, but we also need to pray daily. We are told in the New Testament to "pray without ceasing" (1 Thess 5:17), to pray "at all times in the Spirit" (Eph 6:18), and to pray about everything: "Do not be anxious about anything, but in everything by prayer and supplication with thanksgiving let your requests be made known to God" (Phil 4:6). Prayer is how we "look to the LORD and his strength; seek his face always" (1 Chr 16:11 NIV).

Remember Daniel? When the most famous story about him opens, Daniel is in high favor with King Darius of Babylon (Dan 6:1, 3). Daniel's career was advancing with remarkable success. He had no particular reason to fear, that we know. But he was pursuing God daily in prayer as though he was in continual need. We know this because after his enemies convinced the king to pass an injunction against prayer to anyone except the king, we read, "When Daniel knew that the document had been signed, he went to his house where he had windows in his upper chamber open toward Jerusalem. He got down on his knees three times a day and prayed and gave thanks before his God, as he had done previously" (6:10). This had been Daniel's consistent practice, even

---

4 Smith, *You Are What You Love*, 25.

before the trouble started. When the crisis came, he was prepared for the long dark night in the ground with the hungry beasts.[5]

So to fortify our hearts against fear we need to build Bible reading and prayer into our lives as a daily habit, part of a sacred liturgy that we perform again and again. The second way to pursue these spiritual disciplines is *desperately.*

Have you ever been in the "If you were stuck on a deserted island and could bring one book, what would it be?" conversation? It's always hard to imagine any book other than the Bible not paling on us a bit. Whatever book you bring, whether *Pride and Prejudice* or *War and Peace*, it seems likely that the pages would end up being more useful as fire starters or an emergency food source (in which case, I recommend *War and Peace*). If you don't bring the Bible, it doesn't matter what book you choose. All other books are just books.

In a real sense we are on a deserted island for the rest of our lives—it's called planet Earth. The one book we need for the duration is more than just a book: it's a survival guide. (And it will both get the fire started and be a food source!) We don't read it because that's "what good Christians do." We read it because that's what *desperate* Christians do. If we want victory over fear and anxiety in our lives, if we want to advance into the future with courage, we must cling to the Bible. We must constantly renew and deepen our love for this Book of books. As Moses wrote, "For it is no empty word for you, but your very life, and by this word you shall live long in the land that you are going over the Jordan to possess" (Deut 32:47).

---

5 Daniel credits his deliverance directly to God: "My God sent his angel and shut the lions' mouths, and they have not harmed me, because I was found blameless before him" (Dan 6:21). Josephus, the first-century Jewish historian, wrote in *Jewish Antiquities* 10.11.6 that Daniel's opponents responded by claiming to King Darius that Daniel survived not because God had heard him but because the lions weren't hungry. In his version Darius promptly tested their theory by ordering the lions to be well fed and then throwing in Daniel's enemies. Turns out their theory was false.

By reading the Bible desperately, we are purposefully searching its pages for help. As we read, God gradually transforms us from shaking and scared people into warriors. When Paul urges the Ephesians to "be strong in the Lord and in the strength of his might" he reminds them of everything that they have in Christ using the metaphor of a suit of armor (6:10). According to Paul, believers are belted, plated, shod, helmeted, and shielded (with truth, righteousness, the gospel of peace, faith, and salvation). But only one piece of this spiritual equipment is an actual weapon: an offensive accessory, not a defensive one. Paul wrote, "And take … the sword of the Spirit, which is the word of God" (6:17). That's all we have with which to fight. And, when it's wielded in the Spirit, it's all we need.

Peter also testified that we have everything we need for the fight: "His divine power has granted to us all things that pertain to life and godliness, through the knowledge of him who called us to his own glory and excellence, by which he has granted to us his precious and very great promises" (2 Pet 1:3–4). If we believe God has commanded us not to fear, then we must also believe he has given us what we need in order to obey the command.

As the world gets scarier, the people of God don't stand weaponless. We have the mighty word of God in our hands like a sword. We also have a shield: "In all circumstances take up the shield of faith, with which you can extinguish all the flaming darts of the evil one" (Eph 6:16). Yet my point is, we will only take up the sword of the Spirit and the shield of faith when we realize the seriousness of the spiritual battle that is raging around us and within us. Thus, we must read the Bible with desperation.

We also need to pray desperately. We are meant to bring our fears and needs to God. We don't save prayer for when things are going well; we pray *because* we are afraid. Prayer is the conduit for God's help and comfort to reach us. David knew this. He wrote, "From the end of the earth I call to you *when* my heart is faint" (Ps 61:2). And we have James's counsel: "Is anyone among you in trouble? Let them pray" (5:13 NIV).

Can you hear the desperation in the biblical prayers? Consider: "My Rock, be not deaf to me!" (Ps 28:1) and "Be pleased, O LORD, to deliver me! O LORD, make haste to help me!" (Ps 40:13).

Desperation in a godly sense is a cousin to watchfulness. Jesus exhorted his disciples, "Watch and pray that you may not enter into temptation. The spirit indeed is willing, but the flesh is weak" (Matt 26:41); "But stay awake at all times, praying that you may have strength to escape all these things that are going to take place, and to stand before the Son of Man" (Luke 21:36). Likewise, Paul wrote, "Continue steadfastly in prayer, being watchful in it with thanksgiving" (Col 4:2).

I want our practice of turning to God in prayer to be so automatic, such an ingrained and instinctive response, that, when fear rises and confronts us yet again, we respond immediately with "I know what to do" and we hit our knees. I want us to answer "yes" to the question of Lilias Trotter, "Whatever is the next grace for your soul, can you believe for its supply at once, straight out from the dry, bare need?"[6]

I find it interesting when people say, "Why should I pray? God hasn't answered." If God had fully answered us, would we pray? What reason do we have then to petition the throne? We pray precisely because God hasn't answered yet. (My children usually stop asking me for a snack once they have apples and granola bars in their hands.) When it comes to prayer, we are tempted to use what C. S. Lewis called the "heads I win, tails you lose" argument. In Lewis's epistolary work *The Screwtape Letters*, Screwtape, the senior demon, gives this counsel to his nephew Wormwood, who is assigned to discourage a new Christian from praying:

> If the thing he prays for doesn't happen, then that is
> one more proof that petitionary prayers don't work;
> if it does happen, he will, of course, be able to see
> some of the physical causes which led up to it, and
> "therefore it would have happened anyway," and thus

---

6   Trotter, *Parables of the Cross*, 26.

a granted prayer becomes just as good a proof as a
denied one that prayers are ineffective.[7]

Recognizing this temptation to doubt should make us even more desperate in prayer.

There is a certain ferocity to prayers of faith. We desperately clutch our God when relief hasn't yet been given. We wrestle with him, refusing to let go until he blesses us. Our most desperate moments are the best opportunities for God's love to be poured into us. As Elisabeth Elliot testified,

> The hard place in which you perhaps find yourself is
> the very place in which God is giving you opportunity
> to look only to Him, to spend time in prayer, and to
> learn long-suffering, gentleness, meekness—in short,
> to learn the depths of the love that Christ Himself has
> poured out on all of us.[8]

We need to read the Bible and pray daily, we need to do so desperately—coming with our needs—and, lastly, we need to read and pray *meditatively*. Eugene Peterson wrote, "Reading is an immense gift, but only if the words are assimilated, taken into the soul, eaten, chewed, gnawed, and received in unhurried delight."[9] We must give the text time beyond what it takes to decode words and comprehend sentences. To truly defeat fear whenever it makes its ugly presence known, we want the truths that we read and pray to lodge firmly not just among the facts in our minds but within the passions and affections of our hearts.

I once ate a seven-inch black snake in a restaurant painted red and gold in Wuhan, China. It was a place like a fondue restaurant, where you

7 Lewis, *Screwtape Letters*, 148.

8 Elliot, *Keep a Quiet Heart*, 233.

9 Peterson, *Eat This Book*, 11.

sink your raw food in a boiling vat of spicy broth and cook it for yourself tableside. A sweet Chinese friend cooked the snake for me—indeed, it was her idea. I just trusted her when she said it was ready. Grimace-smiling in feigned anticipation, I chopsticked it into my mouth whole, swallowing it in segments (as I did the spider, see chapter 2). I've been asked more than a few times what that snake tasted like. I think I said, "Chicken." But the truth is, I was a little preoccupied with the process and my surroundings, and, though I may never be presented with that particular culinary experience again in my entire life, I completely forgot to taste it.

Tasting something requires more effort than eating it. You must hold it in your mouth long enough. This is the part I neglected with the black snake. The process of tasting can be rather complex, as initial flavors fade and later, subtler ones develop on your tongue. You quite often have to chew a time or two to release flavor. And you have to pay attention. To get the most from tasting anything, you have to think about what it tastes like.

Similarly, we must engage our brains when we read our Bibles. Oswald Chambers has argued, "The great need for the saint is to get his brains at work on the Word of God, otherwise he will stagnate, no matter how much he may name the Name of God."[10] But there is more to chewing on God's word than consulting commentaries, concordances, and Greek and Hebrew lexicons. If that's all we do, there is a danger that we will forget to read the Bible *meditatively*—what Eugene Peterson has called "formatively, reading in order to live."[11] First and even foremost, our Bibles are living documents written to ordinary people. Use your brain when you can (always a good idea), but don't make reading it merely an intellectual thing. I appreciate biblical scholars and all that they have to teach us. But you don't have to be one for God's word to speak powerfully to you.

---

10 Chambers, *Notes on Isaiah, Jeremiah, and Ezekiel.*

11 Peterson, *Eat This Book*, xi.

I'm by nature a fast reader, but when I come to my Bible these days I try to read with the brakes on. I want to read a line and sit with it, let it "sink in," listen to it with my heart as well as my brain. I want to "*taste* and see that the LORD is good" (Ps 34:8) in its pages. This kind of reading is the *lectio divina* of Christians through the ages—a spiritual reading, a listening reading, a more prayerful reading.

Thus, there is a profound, organic connection between reading the words of Scripture slowly and praying. As we meditate on what we read, it is natural to "pray it in"—to respond to what the Holy Spirit is saying to our hearts in prayer.

> It is a particularly lovely thing to take up an attitude
> of prayer as we hear the Word of God so that we
> can move straight from the Scriptures to talk to our
> Heavenly Father, to the Lord Jesus, and to the Holy
> Spirit, bringing before him the truth he has just
> imported, turning it into prayer, praise, adoration,
> thanksgiving, and intercession.[12]

True meditation is the fusion of the word and prayer. The Puritan Thomas Manton makes this point well:

> Meditation is a sort of middle duty between the word
> and prayer, and hath respect to both. The word feedeth
> meditation, and meditation feedeth prayer. These duties
> must always go hand in hand; meditation must follow
> hearing and precede prayer. To hear and not to meditate
> is unfruitful. We may hear and hear, but it is like putting
> a thing into a bag with holes.... It is rashness to pray
> and not to meditate. What we take in by the word we
> digest by meditation and let out by prayer.[13]

---

12 Motyer, *Loving the Old Testament*, 1.

13 Manton, *Complete Works of Thomas Manton*, 272–73, as quoted by Whitney, *Spiritual Disciplines*, 99.

The struggle with fear is a lifelong battle, reaching an intense pitch in different seasons. We cannot be ready to fight in an instant, but we are prepared by a lifetime of training through the daily disciplines of prayer and Bible reading. The battle is largely won or lost in our ordinary moments of daily devotion. Reading the Scriptures and praying daily, desperately, and meditatively is how to "let the word of Christ dwell in you richly," as Paul exhorted the Colossians (3:16). It isn't about checking boxes, feeling like a good Christian, or virtue signaling. It is the way to keep an armored, anchored, and quieted heart. A quiet heart is the opposite of a heart noisy with anxieties. Such a heart is formed in us as we are reminded of God's love in the pages of the Bible and as we draw near to him in prayer.

Sacred Courage

Discussion Questions

1. Are you in the daily habit of reading the Bible and spending time dedicated to prayer?

2. What is the quality of your reading and prayer times? What would make them better?

3. What verses and promises do you hold to when you feel anxious or afraid?

11

One Another

"Have your instructors taught you why the Spartans
excuse without penalty the warrior who loses his helmet or
breastplate in battle, but punish with loss of all citizenship
rights the man who discards his shield?"

They had, Alexandros replied.

"Because a warrior carries helmet and breastplate for
his own protection, but his shield for the safety of the whole
line."

Dionekes smiled and placed his hand upon his protégé's
shoulder.

"Remember this, young friend. There is a force beyond
fear. More powerful than self-preservation."

—Steven Pressfield, *Gates of Fire*

When our youngest child was five years old, he became afraid to be by
himself, especially at night. Even if the family were all in the next room
(usually making a tremendous din), he didn't like to step into any room
alone. He was always asking someone to go with him. One evening I
overheard him trying to convince one of his sisters to go with him to
get something in the next room. None of them wanted to leave their
activities. I heard his sweet oldest sister ask, "Would it help if I sang
really loud? Should I sing really loud when you go into your room?"
But it was immediately followed by this comment from his other sister:
"But then you won't be able to hear him as he screams from the jaws of
the monster!"

I love this dialogue because it illustrates (in addition to the hilarious
personality of my second daughter) the various helpful and unhelpful
approaches we can have toward one another's fears. Are the things we
say to others when they are afraid helpful and comforting or the reverse?

Sacred Courage

In this chapter I want to consider the role we can play in the faith journey of others (and the role they play in ours) during fearful times. What are the principles of Christian comfort and fellowship, and how do they differ from the world's wisdom? Which are we offering—and receiving? Hopefully this chapter will help us to reflect: How do we typically try to help our fearful friends? What assumptions underlie our efforts? After discerning what we are already doing, we will then evaluate how to respond more in line with biblical truth, resulting in more genuine help and caring.

First, it's countercultural to confess fear at all in our brazen, self-confident age. After all, being afraid is a weakness, and to the world, weaknesses must be camouflaged and compensated for.

But Christians don't need to mask their weaknesses. Indeed, we have a God who flips the worldly system of values on its head:

> God chose what is foolish in the world to shame the
> wise; God chose what is weak in the world to shame
> the strong; God chose what is low and despised in the
> world, even things that are not, to bring to nothing
> things that are, so that no human being might boast in
> the presence of God. (1 Cor 1:27–29)

God has made it clear that he doesn't despise human weakness, and he is not impressed by human strength.

We are not only safe to admit our weaknesses, our fears, and our struggles, but we are encouraged to do so because we are taught to expect God to reveal himself in those places! Look at the example of Paul. He had some great weakness of his own. We don't know what it was, only that he pleaded with God to take it away. In response, he heard this:

> "My grace is sufficient for you, for my power is made
> perfect in weakness." Therefore I will boast all the
> more gladly of my weaknesses, so that the power of
> Christ may rest upon me. For the sake of Christ, then,

> I am content with weaknesses, insults, hardships,
> persecutions, and calamities. For when I am weak,
> then I am strong. (2 Cor 12:9–10)

Remember that fears, though a weakness, are like burdens in this way: they are better shared.

Even in the church, we can be reluctant to share things about ourselves that might make us appear weak in faith or less spiritual than we hope others think we are. We might choose to confide only in professional counselors or therapists because it is safer to be vulnerable with someone who doesn't actually know us. It lowers our risk of harming our own reputations by what we share. There is definitely a need for trained counselors and therapists, and I know their contribution is valuable. But if we never share weaknesses or struggles with one another, our opportunities to grow together with the believers around us, and their opportunities to be encouraged when God works through our weaknesses, are dramatically lessened.

According to the world's wisdom, admitting one's weakness, even to a friend, is risky because it leaves one vulnerable. The other person probably won't mind seeing your weakness because, in a worldly friendship, they might feel stronger in *comparison*. In a worldly friendship, I feel the need to disguise my own weakness, but it might suit me if others appear weak because it may make me appear stronger. This is the zero-sum game that is played by the flesh: I feel stronger when you appear weaker, but if you project strength, I instinctively feel weakness. This is not a game that we have to play!

Paul exhorts us to identify and sympathize ("have fellow feeling") with one another, not to play off of each other. There ought not to be division among the parts of the body of Christ, but rather its members are to have "the same care for one another. If one member suffers, all suffer together; if one member is honored, all rejoice together" (1 Cor 12:25–26). In other words, our emotions are to move in a similar direction—not an opposite one. Newton's third law of motion does not apply when we are hearing each other's fears in the church. Thus, the first principle is that we should be open and honest in admitting our fears in the hope that our vulnerability will be met with sympathy and encouragement.

The second principle, related to the first, is that we are only as strong as the strength we have together. Your courage matters to me, as does the tested genuineness of your faith—and mine matters to you. Look at the metaphor Paul uses for the church when he wrote to the Ephesians:

> So then you are no longer strangers and aliens, but
> you are fellow citizens with the saints and members of
> the household of God, built on the foundation of the
> apostles and prophets, Christ Jesus himself being the
> cornerstone, in whom the *whole structure, being joined
> together*, grows into a holy temple in the Lord. In him
> you also are *being built together* into a dwelling place
> for God by the Spirit. (2:19–22)

We are one interlocking structure, established on the strongest and straightest of stones, Christ Jesus, the cornerstone. No one stone can distinguish itself in comparison to the weakness of stones around it; instead, the whole structure stands or falls together. In Christian friendship and unity, strength is *collective*.

The idea of collective strength can be difficult for us to understand. The communal mindset of the New Testament and the early church clashes with our Western individualism. We are conditioned in a thousand ways to think of ourselves primarily as discrete and autonomous individuals, competing with others. While we may acknowledge our need for other believers and recognize the benefits of the church community for our own personal growth, rarely do we view spiritual growth in corporate terms, as Ephesians 2 encourages us to do. Do we realize we bear a sense of responsibility for one another? Are we conscious of the ways in which we are connected to one another in the mind of God?

Try administering this simple test: Did Jesus teach us to pray, "Give me this day my daily bread" or "Give *us* this day *our* daily bread"?[1] In what kind of mindset do the plural pronouns of Jesus actually make sense? We are fond of claiming God as our Father, but do we as readily comprehend that by the same gift of adoption, you are made my sibling and I am yours?

As I've already mentioned, Christians should freely divulge their fears and expect God's strength to show up in that place. Yet not only that, but we must also realize that we have a vested interest in the faith of one another because we stand together in a single structure, a single body. If we stand, we stand together. If we live, we live together. Paul expressed his solidarity with the Thessalonians in this way:

> But now that Timothy has come to us from you, and has brought us the good news of your faith and love and reported that you always remember us kindly and long to see us, as we long to see you—for this reason, brothers, in all our distress and affliction we have been comforted about you through your faith. For *now we live, if* you are standing fast in the Lord.—(1 Thess 3:6–8)

Paul could have written, "For now we are encouraged, if" or "Now we are relieved, if." Yet by writing "now we *live*, if," Paul was, incredibly, tying his sense of life to the spiritual condition of his beloved friends. Likewise, in battling for the dread-free life, we don't equip ourselves alone and head out to fight our fears guerilla-style, making independent attacks and then vanishing into the jungle. Instead, we march out into the plains in phalanx, with interlocking shields—covering for one another.

---

1 Read Matthew 6:11 or Luke 11:3 to find out.

A third principle: *every one of us* in the body has a specific call to strengthen and support one another in fearful times. This is not only the responsibility of the pastor or the trained counselor. We are not underqualified to walk alongside each other, and it is not someone else's job. It is specifically and scripturally our job. Look at Ephesians 4:11–13:

> And he gave the apostles, the prophets, the evangelists,
> the shepherds and teachers, to equip the saints for the
> work of ministry, for building up the body of Christ,
> until we all attain to the unity of the faith and of the
> knowledge of the Son of God, to mature manhood, to
> the measure of the stature of the fullness of Christ.

Who is doing "the work of ministry, for building up the body of Christ," in these verses? All of the listed vocations—apostles, prophets, evangelists, shepherds, and teachers—are dispensed to equip the saints for the work of ministry. In Christian friendship, building you up is my job, and building me up is yours. It is not only the pastor's job, and it is not "above our paygrade."

Paul goes on to say,

> Speaking the truth in love, we are to grow up in every
> way into him who is the head, into Christ, from
> whom the whole body, joined and held together by
> every joint with which it is equipped, when each part
> is working properly, makes the body grow so that it
> builds itself up in love. (4:15–16)

So there is our call. This means we all have a vocation: speak the truth in love, build up the body in love.

In these verses, Paul urges the Ephesians to speak "the truth in love." Sometimes we use that phrase to emphasize the way in which we should say hard things to each other, if they must be said. While that is certainly true, "the truth in love" doesn't have to mean painful or convicting things. Sometimes the truth that needs to be spoken is utterly comforting. This is the case when we encourage fearful friends with the truths of Scripture. In my experience, though Christians sometimes have to share uncomfortable truths, calling out the lies that fear tells us isn't usually one of these times. The things that fear says to us are what hurt us; it is comforting to hear these held up in the light of God's promises and exposed.

As I've labored against fear I have been helped by insights from sermons or published books. Yet many of the most inspiring and meaningful words I have received have come from the lips of friends in Christ. These sisters and brothers have spoken the most loving truths into my soul, probably because they know me the best, and they want the best for me. So don't underestimate your ability to draw near to your fellow believers and build them up in Christ. With the Holy Spirit of God speaking through you, whether you are a trained counselor or a pastor or not, it may be that God has chosen to use *you* in the life of another for such a time as this.

Others could doubtless add many more to this list, but the fourth and final principle of Christian comfort and fellowship is that we offer one another the comfort we have received from God. (Note: We don't offer statistics, placebos, or our opinions on the world situation.) Our task is to pass on what we've received—the source of comfort is always God; we are the conduit. Paul, in 2 Corinthians 1, prayed these words:

> Blessed be the God and Father of our Lord Jesus
> Christ, the Father of mercies and God of all comfort,
> who comforts us in all our affliction, so that we may
> be able to comfort those who are in any affliction, with
> the comfort with which we ourselves are comforted by
> God. (vv. 3–4)

Note that Paul gave a reason for all the comfort God bestowed on him and Timothy: *so that* they can comfort others. This is one way also in which God redeems our suffering—as we pass through it, we get to know God and his promises better, so we have more to offer when hard times come to others. It is a continual regifting of God's grace and goodness.

In the next verses Paul says,

> For as we share abundantly in Christ's sufferings, so
> through Christ we share abundantly in comfort too.
> If we are afflicted, it is for your comfort and salvation;
> and if we are comforted, it is for your comfort,
> which you experience when you patiently endure
> the same sufferings that we suffer. Our hope for you
> is unshaken, for we know that as you share in our
> sufferings, you will also share in our comfort. (vv. 5–7)

How do these verses connect to fear? As Paul makes clear in the subsequent verses, he had a near-death experience shortly before he wrote the letter. The situation for Paul and Timothy was a scary one. Scholars speculate that they may have faced severe persecution or physical illness. Whatever it was, Paul writes that they "were so utterly burdened beyond our strength that we despaired of life itself" (v. 8) and that they felt that they were under "the sentence of death" (v. 9). In this circumstance, they received the "comfort" of Christ.

Many English translations use the word *comfort* here, while others use the word *consolation*. But the Greek words used here "do not refer to the alleviation of grief or sorrow, as the English word 'comfort' suggests, but they rather refer to strengthening in the midst of adversity."[2] When we read "comfort" here, the sense is that of the Latin *comfortare*, meaning "to strengthen much" and "to encourage."[3]

What Paul and Timothy had received from God was strength and encouragement in their difficult and scary times. Their hardships

---

2 Kirk, *Departure of an Apostle*, 159.

3 Furnish, *II Corinthians*, 109.

weren't removed or even alleviated, but a strengthening took place between them and the believers at Corinth that helped them. Listen to Paul's words later in the letter—the only place he admits to being afraid.

> For when we came into Macedonia, our bodies had
> no rest, but we were afflicted at every turn—fighting
> without and fear within. But God, who comforts the
> downcast, comforted us by the coming of Titus, and
> not only by his coming but also by the comfort with
> which he was comforted by you. (7:5–7)

Paul fought his "fear within" with the encouragement of Titus, who was able to strengthen him in God because he himself had experienced a comfort, or strengthening, from God—and that from the Corinthian believers. God remains the source of all comfort, but what his children receive is being passed on from believer to believer.

There is an Old Testament example of this dynamic between Jonathan and David. David has fled from Saul and taken refuge in the wilderness of Ziph.

> And Jonathan, Saul's son, rose and went to David at
> Horesh, and *strengthened his hand in God*. And he said
> to him, "Do not fear, for the hand of Saul my father
> shall not find you. You shall be king over Israel, and I
> shall be next to you. Saul my father also knows this."
> And the two of them made a covenant before the
> LORD. David remained at Horesh, and Jonathan went
> home. (1 Sam 23:16–18)

Jonathan comes to David at a fearful time, when David is in hiding and in grave danger. How does he strengthen him? He encourages the heart of David not to fear—predicting that David will be preserved and become Israel's king. At first glance, this may seem like Jonathan is confidently promising what he cannot be certain of, just to make David feel better. But remember, at the time when Jonathan spoke these words,

God had already led Samuel to anoint David as the future king of Israel (1 Sam 16:12–13). Jonathan is reminding David of God's promise.

Recently a friend was sharing with me that she has entered a new season of anxiety. Triggered initially by some health concerns, she felt her fears in many areas were suddenly increasing. She told me she was too tense to sleep at night but would stay up alone half the night, feeling fearful. I tried to share with her how God has helped me in this area; how I now try to answer the what-if questions with God's promises. I prayed over her for peace and courage.

The next day she grabbed me at our children's school and said, "I need to show you a video." She held out her phone to show a video of a lion, being chased and harassed by a clan of snarling hyenas. The lion was pressed on all sides. The aggressive hyenas, darting here and there, began to pile on top of the lion and beat it down. Suddenly, a second lion came bounding up and roared loudly at the hyenas, who instantly scattered.

"That was what you did for me yesterday," she said. Really that's what God did for us both. That's what he equips us to do for one another: be the second lion. Bound in, however clumsily, and roar the truth as loud as you can.[4]

These, then, are some guiding principles to consider when we try to encourage one another in times of fear. Admitting fear is both a humble and courageous act, showing a person's willingness to see God's strength triumph instead of their own. We circle the wagons and build up one another when fear makes itself felt among us because what is needed is our collective strength, not an individual opportunity to boast. We each have a vocation to speak the truth in love, building up one another as we all grow up into Christ, who truly leaves no child behind. What we have to offer one another is simply what we receive from God.

---

4 "Now this is the Law of the Jungle—as old and as true as the sky; And the Wolf that shall keep it may prosper, but the Wolf that shall break it must die. As the creeper that girdles the tree-trunk the Law runneth forward and back —For the strength of the Pack is the Wolf, and the strength of the Wolf is the Pack." Kipling, *Second Jungle Book*, ch. 2.

Do you know what this looks like in practice?

When a friend is afraid, how do we "strengthen their hand in God"? According to the first principle, we don't need to hide our weaknesses; it is right for Christians to admit their fears to one another. We must listen to their fears with a humble heart because we too have been afraid. If the particular fear they are dealing with happens to be one we haven't yet faced, it is profoundly unhelpful to say that—its usefulness is roughly on par with my daughter's words about not hearing her brother's cries from the jaws of the monster. Perhaps it's true: maybe, by God's grace, you truly have victory over fear in your life. If that's the case, you should get busy passing on the comfort that you receive from God—the church needs you.

In a conversation about fear, we shouldn't listen with only one part of our minds while the other parts are busy preparing to reason the other person out of her fears, to apply likelihoods or statistics, or to promise them confidently that their fears won't happen. (Remember, that's not what Jonathan was doing—he was reminding David of God's promise.) These are worldly reactions to fear, not Christian ones. If we want to strengthen a friend's hand in God, we also don't try to convict or accuse them of sin because they are fearful or "not trusting God enough." As we've seen, fear does lead us to sinful responses and attitudes, but being accused or shamed for it will not encourage anyone.

Putting the second principle in practice, the idea that our strength is collective, means that the goal of the conversation is to build up the other person, and not always with a flood of words. My mother tells a story about a fearful time when she was deeply encouraged by four words. Mom has a deep, gut-clenching fear of flying. But I was about to have a baby on the other side of the Atlantic, and I needed her to come and be with me. In the weeks before the flight, Mom was really struggling with the upcoming journey. When she told a Christian friend about it, her friend said quietly, "Jean, you can do this." Suddenly, Mom says, she knew that she could. This is not an example of a friend lecturing my mom about a biblical promise. Her friend was just speaking the truth in love. My mom could make the flight and she did.

Sacred Courage

Here is a final story to illustrate the third and fourth principles: I was sitting in my parents' church in Denver, just weeks after I'd had a stroke and we'd suddenly left Indonesia. Suddenly during the sermon, the right side of my body went numb, my tongue went numb, there was a loud roaring in my ears, I couldn't breathe in, and my vision clouded. The pastor up front looked like a wiggly cartoon. My brain was screaming, It's happening again, it's happening again! I grabbed my husband's arm with my left hand, and when his concerned face turned, I frantically peered at his expression in order to read if I was having another stroke or if this was just my brain processing trauma once again. Based on his calm reaction I told myself it was PTSD and quietly left the room, sinking into a chair alone in the lobby.

The attack left me shaking and confused, one side of my body still numb. I sat there, I hoped normally, while internally screaming for God to help me. I felt like I would never be okay again. My whole life had shrunk to this constant internal battle with fear and trauma, and I did not want to live it anymore.

There was a touch on my shoulder. I turned to see the face of a woman I had met just weeks previously. She placed something in my hand and said quietly, "I am praying for you," and stepped away. I don't know if I answered her or was able to muster up my polite church mask in time or not. I rather think not. I looked down at what she had put in my hand. It was a round medallion on a chain. I turned it over, and read these words: *Courage, dear heart.*

It came from a woman who once opened her door to find police officers there to tell her of the tragic death of her young husband. She didn't know much beyond the broad outline of my story, and she couldn't have known the depths of my internal terror at that moment. But she knew about the comfort she had received from God.

Courage, dear heart. Courage. That was what she wished on me, pressing it lovingly into my hands. It wasn't a judgment, a lecture, or a boast. It was a benediction.

Discussion Questions

1. When have others come around you with encouragement at key times when you needed it?

2. What role do you believe God wants us to play in the journey of others?

3. Who in your life needs *encouragement* right now? Who needs prayer as they battle fear or anxiety?

12

A Call to Christian Courage

Lucy leant her head on the edge of the fighting-top and whispered, "Aslan, Aslan, if ever you loved us at all, send us help now." The darkness did not grow any less, but she began to feel a little—a very, very little—better. "After all, nothing has really happened to us yet," she thought.

"Look!" cried Rynelf's voice hoarsely from the bows. There was a tiny speck of light ahead, and while they watched a broad beam of light fell from it upon the ship. It did not alter the surrounding darkness, but the whole ship was lit up as if by searchlight. Caspian blinked, stared round, saw the faces of his companions all with wild, fixed expressions. Everyone was staring in the same direction: behind everyone lay his black, sharply edged shadow.

Lucy looked along the beam and presently saw something in it. At first it looked like a cross, then it looked like an aeroplane, then it looked like a kite, and at last with a whirring of wings it was right overhead and was an albatross. It circled three times round the mast and then perched for an instant on the crest of the gilded dragon at the prow. It called out in a strong sweet voice what seemed to be words though no one understood them. After that it spread its wings, rose, and began to fly slowly ahead, bearing a little to starboard. Drinian steered after it not doubting that it offered good guidance. But no one except Lucy knew that as it circled the mast it had whispered to her, "Courage, dear heart," and the voice, she felt sure, was Aslan's, and with a delicious smell breathed in her face.

In a few moments the darkness turned into a grayness ahead, and then, almost before they dared to begin hoping, they had shot out into the sunlight and were in the warm, blue world again.

—C. S. Lewis, *The Voyage of the Dawn Treader*

Sacred Courage

Plutarch, in his collection of biographies of ancient Romans titled *The Fall of the Roman Republic*, wrote a story about Pompey the Great, the Roman general at the time of Julius Caesar.[1] While amassing his soldiers for a great battle, Pompey became fearful that the initial charge would scatter his front lines, dissipating his forces too early in the struggle. So he gave the unusual order for his men to stand still in their places, holding out their spears, and to wait for the enemy while rooted to the spot. Though his military might was far superior to his enemy's, when the charge came, Pompey's men were overrun. Plutarch wrote,

> According to Caesar, Pompey made a mistake in adopting these tactics. He says that their effect was to deprive the blows of the force which they would have had if the soldiers had charged forward; that this running to meet the enemy, with the shouting and the actual physical motion, is usually the most important factor of all in promoting the right kind of enthusiasm and élan in battle; and that Pompey sacrificed these advantages by fixing his men to the spot where they were standing and so chilling their ardour.[2]

In this battle, Pompey's troops should have surged forward to victory, but instead, they stood still. Likewise, in the battle against fear, merely taking up a defensive stance is not enough, we must *charge*. If our fear keeps us rooted in place, it keeps us from stepping out in obedience. So as we dismantle our fears with the love and promises of God, we must also cultivate a heart of Christian courage.

The best definition of Christian courage I have ever found comes from a sermon delivered in 1642 by Simeon Ash, under the laborious title "Sermon Preached before the Commanders of the Military Forces

---

1 Pompey was the general responsible for the invasion of Jerusalem and the incorporation of Judea into the Roman Republic in 63 BC.

2 Plutarch, *Fall of the Roman Republic*, 231.

of the Renowned Citie of London." Ash wrote, "Christian courage may be thus described. It is the undaunted audacity of a sanctified heart in adventuring upon difficulties and undergoing hardships for a good cause upon the call of God."[3] As this book concludes, let's look at three different parts of this definition, considering how Ash's insights can help us cultivate Christian courage.

The first phrase to ponder is Ash's reference to "undaunted audacity." Notice that in the entire definition, there is no reference to fear or the measure of it that may be present. This suggests that you can be fearful and yet simultaneously "undaunted." Merriam-Webster's dictionary defines undaunted as "courageously resolute especially in the face of danger or difficulty: not discouraged." Dictionary.com defines it as "undiminished in courage or valor; not giving way to fear; intrepid." Fear is present, but so is audacity.

The word *audacity* is one of two words in this definition that suggest boldness to me. The second one is "adventuring." Both words suggest acting with confidence, striding forward to meet what challenges there are. It is the kind of approach in Hebrews 4:16: "Let us then with confidence draw near to the throne of grace, that we may receive mercy and find grace to help in time of need." The cross has not only given us the confidence to approach God,[4] but also because of the cross we have the confidence to witness boldly to our world—even when it's dangerous. As Paul wrote to the Thessalonians, "But though we had already suffered and been shamefully treated at Philippi, as you know, we had boldness in our God to declare to you the gospel of God in the midst of much conflict" (1 Thess 2:2). Don't think that Paul uses the phrase "much conflict" lightly here. In Philippi, Paul and Silas were dragged into the marketplace, their clothes ripped from them, and their bodies bloodied with rods. Then they were thrown into prison.[5] Yet throughout it all

3 Simeon Ash, as quoted by Spurgeon, *Treasury of David*, 2:77.
4 See Ephesians 3:12.
5 See Acts 16.

Paul and Silas had boldness in God to adventure upon difficulties.

In another place, writing about his hope in Christ, Paul explains his boldness:

> Such is the confidence that we have through Christ
> toward God. Not that we are sufficient in ourselves to
> claim anything as coming from us, but our sufficiency
> is from God, who has made us sufficient to be
> ministers of a new covenant, not of the letter but of
> the Spirit. For the letter kills, but the Spirit gives life.
> (2 Cor 3:4–6)

Paul's courage and confidence were the fruits of his belief in the promises (or "covenant") of God, coming true through Christ. He is clear that this boldness isn't something he has somehow mustered up within himself, but rather, it is gifted by the Holy Spirit to enable his obedience to the ministry to which God has called him.[6] A few verses later, Paul writes, "Since we have such a hope, we are very bold" (3:12).

Hope is the reason our audacity is "undaunted." The hope that we have reminds us that, whatever the short-term cost, ultimately, we cannot lose. If we do not cling to anything but Christ, the loss of anything but Christ cannot "daunt" us. This, as we grow in it day by day, slowly translates into audacious courage.

G. K. Chesterton explains Christian courage in similar terms, almost as a reckless confidence, in his book *Orthodoxy*: "Courage is almost a contradiction in terms. It means a strong desire to live taking the form of a readiness to die." Chesterton goes on to show how sometimes being ready to die helps a person take significant risks to stay alive:

> This paradox is the whole principle of courage; even
> of quite earthly or quite brutal courage. A man cut
> off by the sea may save his life if he will risk it on

---

6 Referred to also in Ash's definition as "upon the call of God."

the precipice. He can only get away from death by continually stepping within an inch of it. A soldier surrounded by enemies, if he is to cut his way out, needs to combine a strong desire for living with a strange carelessness about dying. He must not merely cling to life, for then he will be a coward, and will not escape. He must not merely wait for death, for then he will be a suicide, and will not escape. He must seek his life in a spirit of furious indifference to it; he must desire life like water and yet drink death like wine.

The paradoxical nature of courage that Chesterton notes here accords with what I wrote in chapter 4 about the fear of death. We will never be filled with an undaunted audacity in life if we are not, in one sense, indifferent to death. Chesterton continues:

No philosopher, I fancy, has ever expressed this romantic riddle with adequate lucidity, and I certainly have not done so. But Christianity has done more: it has marked the limits of it in the awful graves of the suicide and the hero, showing the distance between him who dies for the sake of living and him who dies for the sake of dying. And it has held up ever since above the European lances the banner of the mystery of chivalry: the Christian courage, which is a disdain of death; not the Chinese courage, which is a disdain of life.[7]

We can check Chesterton's idea of Christian courage as a disdain for death against the exhortations of the apostle Paul. Paul could undergo hardships in the calling God gave him because, for him, death was gain. He wrote,

---

7   Chesterton, *Orthodoxy*, 102.

Sacred Courage

> So we are always of good courage. We know that while
> we are at home in the body we are away from the
> Lord, for we walk by faith, not by sight. Yes, we are of
> good courage, and we would rather be away from the
> body and at home with the Lord. So whether we are at
> home or away, we make it our aim to please him.
> (2 Cor 5:6–9)

How can we cultivate courage? If we "walk by faith," if we are clinging to the hope we have in Christ, if we would rather be "at home with the Lord," we have already begun.

Courage is not only manifested in life-or-death situations. By Ash's definition, all difficulties and hardships undertaken for Christ would fall into the category of courageous "adventures" (even the kind of adventures Paul and Silas had in Philippi). Right now, by the call of God, I live in a small town in Southeast Asia. The difficulties and hardships that come with this call mean that during the night I will have to attend the funeral of a much-loved uncle online, rather than gathering with my family in person. Today's hardship adventures also include finding thick layers of white mold growing on our clothes, the presence of a crazed bat living in the rafters in our living room, and waking up this morning to dozens of terribly itchy bites and finding our third pervasive bedbug infestation in less than a year. Part of me would like to quit the call of God pronto. But I want the undaunted audacity of those whose all is Christ. "The righteous are bold as a lion" (Prov 28:1). So I'm going after those bedbugs like a lion. (I will probably let Alex go after the bat. I want him to have undaunted audacity, too.)

We fight *differently*. We "adventure upon difficulties" and "undergo hardships" differently if our banners bear God's name, if we are confident in the victorious second coming of Christ. Our afflictions become "light" and "momentary" in comparison to what we will gain then (2 Cor 4:17). Like the Hebrew believers in the first century, we will be courageous because of the knowledge we have been given of what is to come. The author of Hebrews wrote to them, "For you had compassion on those in prison, and you joyfully accepted the plundering of your property, since you knew that you yourselves had a better possession and an abiding one" (10:34). Future gains sustain them through present losses. The author continues,

> For you have need of endurance, so that when you
> have done the will of God you may receive what is
> promised. For, "Yet a little while, and the coming one
> will come and will not delay; but my righteous one
> shall live by faith, and if he shrinks back, my soul has
> no pleasure in him." (10:36–37)

These verses add another motivation: we cultivate Christian courage because it gives pleasure to the soul of God. Do you see it there in the text? God will greatly reward our confidence, and we will receive what is promised. This knowledge, and the faith it takes to act upon it, results in Christian courage.

Another phrase in Simeon Ash's definition to meditate upon is "a sanctified heart." What does sanctification have to do with courage? As Ash asserts, Christian courage is "the undaunted audacity of a sanctified heart in adventuring upon difficulties and undergoing hardships for a good cause upon the call of God." Dear heart, if you are trusting Christ, that is you. Sanctification is one of those realities that has both *then* and *now* aspects to it. Are we really sanctified—"set apart as holy"—now? We are. We read in 1 Corinthians 6:11, "But you were washed, you were sanctified, you were justified in the name of the Lord Jesus Christ and by the Spirit of our God." It is finished.

But in another sense, sanctification is also an ongoing process. When we trusted Christ, he began to transform our hearts and minds, our values and desires. "He who began a good work in you will bring it to completion at the day of Jesus Christ" (Phil 1:6). Christian courage is being built in us as we face our fears. In fact, fear is necessary for courage to be forged. Therefore, we should view sanctification both as the prerequisite for Christian courage and as the process by which it is formed. We will never be courageous in a truly God-honoring way if we are not first sanctified by him. And we will be sanctified by him as we walk forward in faith.

This phrase "sanctified heart" also reminds us that we do not face fears, hardships, and difficulties alone, with recourse only to our own resources. If we did, "undaunted audacity" would be an unfounded and foolish self-confidence. What we have is so much better: a confidence based on the presence of Christ. We don't have to be sufficient to face all things—*he is*. We just hold on to him. He is already in the boat with us as the winds whip up. We must simply cry out to him and rely on his presence. As the thunder booms and the waves beat against us, we may join the psalmist's triumphant declaration: "Whom have I in heaven but you? And there is nothing on earth that I desire besides you. My flesh and my heart may fail, but God is the strength of my heart and my portion forever" (Ps 73:25–26).[8] This is the battle cry of the sanctified heart.

Christian courage is not a particular gift or personality trait that some have and some don't. It is, as Simeon Ash wrote in that sermon almost four hundred years ago, "a virtue theological, as a gracious qualification, put upon the people of God by special covenant."[9] In short, it is a quality growing in the sanctified heart. The heart that trusts in the victory of Christ, the heart that finds its comfort in him, will become courageous and venture forth on God's call.

The final phrase of this definition to consider is "for a good cause upon the call of God." There are as many good causes around us as there

---

8 The psalmist goes on to write, "But for me, it is good to be near God; I have made the Lord God my refuge, that I may tell of all your works" (73:28).

9 Simeon Ash, as quoted by Spurgeon, *Treasury of David*, 2:77.

are wrongs waiting to be put right. But the cause that we adopt, the one for which we really work, is the one to which we are called by God. God's call is what gives our cause significance. His marching orders make our work meaningful.

God's call is also what gives significance to our suffering—our "adventuring upon difficulties and undergoing hardships." Listen closely: we don't suffer just to suffer. When we read the Bible carefully, we must inevitably conclude that suffering is a part of the Christian life, however fearful of it we may be. But we mustn't stop there. We must not neglect the truth that suffering, hardships, difficulties, and fears are only the necessary means to an end, and that end is the glory of God and his coming kingdom. God is glorified in *how* we face these things—he is glorified by our courage.

This means that we are not just enduring and biding time until the Lord returns. Every day that we wait and work is important. If the days were not important, if how we walk as we wait was not significant, if there was no purpose in our suffering, Jesus would have come already. This is the implication of Paul's words to the Corinthians, explaining to them that he did not lose heart because "this light momentary affliction is preparing for us an eternal weight of glory beyond all comparison, as we look not to the things that are seen but to the things that are unseen. For the things that are seen are transient, but the things that are unseen are eternal" (2 Cor 4:17–18). Affliction prepares glory for us.

Paul had found such significance in the call of God that he was able to view his truly hard and formidable circumstances as "light" and "momentary" hardships. (In the same chapter he says, "We are afflicted in every way, but not crushed; perplexed, but not driven to despair; persecuted, but not forsaken; struck down, but not destroyed," vv. 8–9.) Worldly courage is reck*less*, but Christian courage results from a true reckoning, or summing up, of the battle viewed in light of eternity.

We have noted that "do not be afraid" appears many times in Scripture. This exhortation usually appears along with two other things:

nearly always with the assurance of the presence of God and often in the context of something God is calling the recipient to do. This pattern is seen in Deuteronomy 31:6, where the people are being called to invade Canaan and take the land the Lord has given to them: "Be strong and courageous. Do not fear or be in dread of them, for it is the LORD your God who goes with you. He will not leave you or forsake you." When we are called to action by God, we are promised that he will be with us. The call of God is not a single lightning bolt experience followed by divine silence as we struggle to obey. It is a constant whisper as he gently leads us onward, empowering us by the presence of his Holy Spirit. There are none more courageous than those who have God's voice constantly in their ears.

The ongoing call of God not only directs our adventures but sustains them. His presence is the key to courage and the key to our comfort, just as it was for Corrie ten Boom.[10] She wrote, "Every day of my life has ended like this: that deep, steady voice, that sure and eager confiding of my all to the care of God."[11] God's voice is both the spur and the balm as we charge forward with him in this beautiful, significant, glorious life he has given us in Christ.

So take courage, dear heart. Venture forth, undaunted, to lead the life to which you have been called. Our Jesus has said to us, "Fear not, little flock, for it is your Father's good pleasure to give you the kingdom" (Luke 12:32). The kingdom comes.

---

10 Ten Boom endured the horrors of Nazi-occupied Holland and Nazi concentration camps, going on to forgive her captors and testify to God's faithfulness to her in sixty-four countries.

11 Corrie ten Boom, *The Hiding Place*, 149.

Surely goodness and mercy shall follow me
all the days of my life,
and I shall dwell in the house of the LORD forever.

Psalm 23:6

Acknowledgments

I would like to thank Walt Hastings, whose wise and faithful coaching enabled me to finally put this book to paper. Also special thanks to Christine Leverette and Chris McGarvey for their contributions and feedback. I have loved working with William Carey Publishing. Many thanks to Vivian for looking at the manuscript of a new writer.

My dear mother encouraged me constantly throughout the project, but as I have long known that it is impossible to thank her for all she has been and done for me, I will just say here that I thank God for her every day.

Most of all, thanks to Alex, who walks beside me, my true and faithful partner in this and all things. He faithfully led and supported me as I learned every lesson in this book the hard way—and he helped me write them down. His fingerprints are on every single page of every single draft. Having him as my husband is my most precious earthly gift.

Bibliography

Alcorn, Randy. *If God Is Good: Faith in the Midst of Suffering and Evil.* Colorado Springs, CO: Multnomah, 2009.

Arnold, Clinton E. *Ephesians.* Zondervan Exegetical Commentary on the New Testament 10. Grand Rapids: Zondervan, 2010.

Austen, Jane. *Pride and Prejudice.* New York: Penguin, 2008.

Boswell, James. *The Life of Samuel Johnson LL.D.* 3 vols. London: T. Nelson and Sons, 1923.

Bronte, Charlotte. *Jane Eyre.* New York: Harper Press, 2010.

Browning, Robert. *Men and Women.* London: Chapman & Hall, 1855.

Calvin, John. *Commentary on the Book of Psalms.* Translated by James Anderson. Bellingham, WA: Logos Bible Software, 2010.

Calvin, John. *Commentary on the Gospel according to John.* Translated by William Pringle. Bellingham, WA: Logos Bible Software, 2010.

Chambers, Oswald. *Notes on Isaiah, Jeremiah, and Ezekiel.* Grand Rapids: Our Daily Bread Publishing, 2015.

Chesterton, G. K. *Orthodoxy.* Delhi: Grapevine India, 2023.

Dante. *The Divine Comedy, Part 2: Purgatory.* Translated by Dorothy Sayers. New York: Penguin, 1955.

Donne, John. "Meditation Seventeen." In *Devotions upon Emergent Occasions.* 1623.

Donne, John. *The Works of John Donne.* London: John W. Parker, 1839.

Elliot, Elisabeth. *Keep a Quiet Heart.* Ann Arbor, MI: Servant Publications, 1996.

Elliot, Elisabeth. *Through Gates of Splendor.* Carol Stream, IL: Tyndale Momentum, 1996.

ESV Study Bible. Wheaton, IL: Crossway, 2008.

Fuller, Thomas. *The Cause and Cure of a Wounded Conscience.* 1647.

Furnish, Victor Paul. *II Corinthians.* Anchor Bible 32A. Garden City, NY: Doubleday, 1984.

Jacob, Alan. *Breaking Bread with the Dead: A Reader's Guide to a More Tranquil Mind.* New York: Penguin, 2020.

Josephs, Ray. "Robert Frost's Secret." *This Week Magazine*, September 1954.

Kidner, Derek. *Psalms 1–72: An Introduction and Commentary.* Tyndale Old Testament Commentaries 15. Downers Grove, IL: InterVarsity Press, 1973.

Kipling, Rudyard. *The Second Jungle Book.* 1895.

Kirk, Alexander N. *The Departure of an Apostle: Paul's Death Anticipated and Remembered.* Wissenschaftliche Untersuchungen zum Neuen Testament, 2nd ser., 406. Tübingen: Mohr Siebeck, 2015.

Lewis, C. S. *Reflections on the Psalms.* New York: HarperCollins, 2017.

Lewis, C. S. *The Screwtape Letters.* San Francisco: HarperOne, 2009.

Lincoln, A. T. *The Gospel according to St. John.* London: Continuum, 2005.

Lindbergh, Anne Morrow. *Gift from the Sea.* New York: Pantheon, 1955.

Macfarlane, Robert. *Mountains of the Mind: Adventures in Reaching the Summit.* New York: Vintage Books, 2004.

Manton, Thomas. *The Complete Works of Thomas Manton, vol. 17.* Reprint. Worthington, PA: Maranatha Publications, 1970.

Motyer, Alec. *A Christian's Pocket Guide to Loving the Old Testament.* Fearn, UK: Christian Focus Publications, 2015.

Muller, Roland. *Honor and Shame: Unlocking the Door.* Self-published, Xlibris, 2000.

Peterson, Andrew. "Is He Worthy." 2018. CCLI Song #7108951.

Peterson, Eugene H. *Eat This Book.* Grand Rapids: Eerdmans, 2006.

Peterson, Eugene H. *The Message.* Colorado Springs, CO: NavPress, 2018.

Peterson, Jordan B. "Maps of Meaning 11: The Flood and the Tower." May 18, 2017. https://www.youtube.com/watch?v=T4fjSrVCDvA.

Piper, John. *Desiring God: Meditations of a Christian Hedonist.* Colorado Springs, CO: Multnomah, 2003.

Plutarch, *Fall of the Roman Republic.* Translated by Rex Warner. New York: Penguin, 1972.

Bibliography

Ryken, Leland. *The Devotional Poetry of Donne, Herbert, and Milton.* Wheaton, IL: Crossway, 2014.

Shakespeare, William. *Julius Caesar.*

Shakespeare, William. *Much Ado about Nothing.*

Smith, James K. A. *You Are What You Love: The Spiritual Power of Habit.* Grand Rapids: Brazos, 2016.

Spurgeon, Charles H. *The Treasury of David.* 3 vols. Peabody, MA: Hendrickson, 2011.

ten Boom, Corrie. *Clippings from My Notebook.* Nashville: Nelson, 1982.

Tolkien, J. R. R. *The Two Towers.* New York: Ballantine, 1994.

Tolstoy, Leo. *Anna Karenina.* New York: Penguin, 2004.

Tozer, A. W. *The Knowledge of the Holy.* New York: HarperCollins, 1961.

Tripp, Paul David. *New Morning Mercies: A Daily Gospel Devotional.* Wheaton, IL: Crossway, 2014.

Trotter, I. Lilias. *Parables of the Cross.* Fort Myers, FL: Oxvision Books, 2015. First published 1895 by Marshall Brothers (London).

Walton, John H. *Ancient Near Eastern Thought and The Old Testament: Introducing the Conceptual World of the Hebrew Bible.* 2nd ed. Grand Rapids: Baker Academic, 2018.

Warfield, Benjamin B. "The Emotional Life of our Lord." In *The Person and Work of Christ.* Philadelphia: Presbyterian & Reformed, 1950.

Waring, Anna Letitia. *Hymns and Meditations.* 4th ed. London: W. & F. G. Cash, 1854.

Warren, Tish Harrison. *Liturgy of the Ordinary: Sacred Practices in Everyday Life.* Downers Grove, IL: InterVarsity Press, 2016.

Whitney, Donald S. *Spiritual Disciplines for the Christian Life.* 20th-anniversary ed. Colorado Springs, CO: NavPress, 2014.

Wright, N. T. *Paul and the Faithfulness of God.* Christian Origins and the Question of God 4. Minneapolis: Fortress, 2013.

Great Commission Spirituality:
Abiding in Christ, Serving in Obscurity

E. D. Burn By emphasizing that Christ lives in and works through us, Burns reassures readers that true fruitfulness in ministry comes from abiding in Christ, who orchestrates our work by his Word and perfect timing. This resource offers a robust theological framework paired with practical applications.

Facing Fear: The Journey to Mature Courage
in Risk and Persecution

Anna Hampton

This book is a practical guide for believers who long to have bold, mature courage. Cultivating this courage is necessary to endure wisely for Christ's sake. Learning to face our fears, name them, and manage them requires learning specific steps to reduce their impact on us.

Downward Discipleship: How Amy Carmichael Gave
Me Courage to Serve in a Slum

Anita Rahma

Downward Discipleship beckons you to learn from Amy's life—a beacon that questions the cost of true discipleship in our world of pain and injustice. Rahma weaves in her own stirring narrative from Jakarta's slums, presenting a model of discipleship that is demanding as it is rewarding, challenging as it is inspiring.

WILLIAM CAREY PUBLISHING

visit us at missionbooks.org